Sound Systems

Explicit, Systematic Phonics in Early Literacy Contexts

Anna Lyon
Assistant Professor, East Carolina University

Paula Moore
Director and Coordinator, Center for Early Literacy, University of Maine

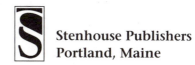

Stenhouse Publishers
Portland, Maine

Stenhouse Publishers
www.stenhouse.com

Credit
Page 32: From *Crabs, Shrimps, and Lobsters* by Stanley L. Swartz. Illustrated by Robert I. Yin. Copyright © 1997. Reprinted with permission of Dominie Press, Inc.

Library of Congress Cataloging-in-Publication Data
Lyon, Anna.
    Sound systems: explicit, systematic phonics in early literacy contexts / Anna Lyon, Paula Moore.
        p. cm.
        Includes bibliographical references (p.) and index.
        ISBN 1-57110-346-5 (alk. paper)
        1. Reading—Phonetic method. 2. Reading (Early childhood) I. Moore, Paula (Paula F.) II. Title.
LB1050.34.L96 2003
372.46'5—dc21   2002026821

Cover photography by Andrew Edgar

Manufactured in the United States of America on acid-free paper
08 07 06 05 04   9 8 7 6 5 4 3 2

To Matthew, Joey, Ben, and Collin and all the children who have taught us so much.

Contents

Preface

Learning to read is a complex process that involves the integration of many cognitive, motor, and perceptual abilities. In this book we focus on the narrow domain of phonics instruction. We are concerned that as the cry for systematic phonics instruction becomes louder and louder at the national level, there may be a tendency in some schools for systematic phonics to be interpreted as "skill 'n drill" or back-to-the-workbook activities. There may also be a tendency for teachers and administrators, anxious to meet the demands of politicians, to adopt fixed-sequence, commercial phonics programs, ignoring that some children know a great deal about phonics before they start school, and some children know very little.

We were both first-grade teachers for some time before moving to university teaching. We both taught phonics from workbooks in a fixed sequence prescribed by the publisher. We know first-hand that fixed-sequence phonics instruction worked for some learners, but not for many others.

The purpose of our book is to support teachers who know that a fixed-sequence phonics program cannot possibly fit all learners. We propose phonics instruction that is explicit, systematic, grounded in research, and taught in authentic early literacy contexts across the literacy block and content areas.

Throughout the book we give examples of classrooms where teachers are teaching phonics systematically and explicitly, not as an add-on but as part of their comprehensive approach to literacy instruction. Children in these classrooms are learning how to use phonics to read and write.

Research on Phonics

Some Clues from Research to Guide Phonics Curriculum, Assessment, and Instruction

The effects of systematic early phonics instruction were significant and substantial in kindergarten and the 1st grade, indicating that systematic phonics programs should be implemented at those age and grade levels.

(NICHHD 2000a, p. 10)

As we walk into Ms. Chandler's kindergarten classroom, we hear the class participating in a shared book reading session enthusiastically chanting:

Run, run,
As fast as you can.
You can't catch me.
I'm the Gingerbread Man!

The children eagerly follow Ms. Chandler's pointer with their eyes as character after character in *The Gingerbread Man* (Parkes and Smith 1986) is taunted by the refrain. A shared reading session is under way, and every child in the class is engaged in the rereading of this long-time favorite book.

Explicit, Systematic Teaching of Letters, Sounds, and Words

After the book has been read and enjoyed, Ms. Chandler says, "We're going to look for words in the story that begin with the letter *m*. Whose name begins with *m*?" Several hands in the group shoot up—Manuel's, Melissa's, and Tammy's. "Let's see, we have Manuel and Melissa. Let's listen to the *M* sound at the beginning of their names." Ms. Chandler and the class say the names slowly several times. "And you are right, Tammy, you have *m*'s in the middle of your name." Ms. Chandler ignores the fact that she asked for names beginning with *m*, and uses this opportunity to extend the learning to *m* sounds in the middle of words. "Let's say Tammy's name slowly and listen for those *m*'s in the middle."

Ms. Chandler asks Manuel, Melissa, and Tammy to point to their names on the name chart, a large chart with all children's first names arranged in rows under large letters. (See Chapter 7 for an example of a name chart.) Ms. Chandler directs the children's attention to the *M/m*'s in the names with her pointer. Next, Ms. Chandler uses her pointer to direct the children's attention to the uppercase and lowercase *m* at the top of the *M* row and instructs the children to find all the uppercase and lowercase *m*'s in the Gingerbread Man story. The children search eagerly and highlight *M/m*s with green highlighter tape. Then, Ms. Chandler reaches for her pointer and again invites the children to read the story with her, pausing to emphasize the highlighted *m* sounds in some words.

As the last chorus finishes, Ms. Chandler quickly reaches for a small white board and demonstrates how to write *M, m,* describing how her pen moves as she does so. She has the children practice writing *M, m* in the air and on each other's backs. In this brief and engaging lesson, Ms. Chandler is using explicit, systematic instruction to help the kindergartners learn about letters, sounds, and words (phonics!) in the context of big book reading.

The Differences Among Phonological Awareness, Phonemic Awareness, and Phonics

Many educational publishers have been swept up in the phonics and phonemic awareness wave. The terms *phonological awareness, phonemic awareness,* and *systematic phonics* turn up in a confusing array of journal articles and titles of commercial programs. However, it is important to understand that these three instructional areas are not the same at all.

And they should be taught in different ways, depending on the learners' varying levels of literacy experience.

Phonological Awareness

Phonological awareness involves an appreciation of the sounds, as well as the meanings, of spoken words. Note that phonological awareness has nothing to do with letters; it is all about sounds. Ms. Chandler could teach phonological awareness during a shared reading of *The Gingerbread Man* (Parkes and Smith 1986) in several ways. Children could listen for the rhyming words, such as *man* and *can*. During a subsequent reading, the children might divide the words by syllables or smaller clusters (*m/an* and *c/an*), and put them back together again. At another time, Ms. Chandler and the children might notice groups of words that have the same beginning (*can't/catch*) or ending (*catch/watch*).

Phonemic Awareness

Phonemic awareness involves teaching children to focus on and manipulate phonemes in spoken syllables and words. Phonemic awareness is a more advanced form of phonological awareness; it involves the understanding that speech can be broken into small units of sound. Children with phonemic awareness can isolate the individual sounds in words. For example, in the word *came,* they can say *c/a/m* as separate sounds, or they can say *cat* without the /c/. Again, phonemic awareness is about sounds, not letters. However, phonemic awareness is important to reading because phonemes are represented by letters. Even three- and four-year-olds can be taught to listen for phonemes in words. Ms. Chandler will find many opportunities to foster phonemic awareness using a variety of quality big books and shared reading experiences. However, phonemic awareness instruction does not constitute a complete reading program, and phonemic awareness instruction is seldom appropriate beyond the first half of kindergarten for typically progressing students. To be useful in reading and writing, phonemic awareness must transition into phonics instruction.

Phonics

The primary focus of phonics instruction is to help beginning readers understand how letters are linked to sounds (phonemes) to form letter-sound correspondences and spelling patterns for use in their reading and writing. Note that you can be sure phonics instruction is going on if letters, not just sounds, are involved in the activity. In the kindergarten example at the beginning of the chapter, Ms. Chandler was providing phonics instruction; she was teaching children to match a sound (phoneme at the beginning of *Manuel* and *Melissa* and the phoneme in the middle of *Tammy*) to the letter *m*.

What the Research Says

Children who are likely to meet success in learning to read in the early grades are those who begin school with knowledge of letters, phonological sensitivity, familiarity with the basic purposes and mechanisms of reading, and language ability (Snow, Burns, and Griffin 1998). The experts agree that, once they are in school, children who receive instruction in phonics, along with a complete reading program including instruction in comprehension and fluency, are more likely to succeed in learning to read and write (Adams 1990; Burns, Griffin, and Snow 1999; Cunningham 1995; Fox 2000; Fountas and Pinnell 1996; Moustafa 1997; NICHHD 2000a and b; Snow, Burns, and Griffin 1998).

But Phonics Is Not So Simple

Researchers in the 1960s established that very few letters in English can be mapped reliably to just one sound (Bailey 1967; Burmeister 1968; Clymer 1963; Emans 1967). For example, even the fairly predictable letter *d* is pronounced /d/ in *leaned* but /t/ in *laughed*. Another fairly predictable letter, *s*, is pronounced /s/ in *list* but /z/ in *says*. Vowels are enormously unpredictable. The letter *a* is represented by a different sound in each of these words: *ant, want, again,* and *cake*. Just the long /a/ sound itself can be written at least three ways as in *tame, rain,* and *weigh*. In one of the early phonics studies Horn (1929) found that there are eighteen sounds associated with the letter *a* in materials that a typical first grader might read!

Berdiansky, Cronnell, and Koehler (1969) examined more than six thousand one- and two-syllable words in the comprehension vocabularies of children ages six to nine. They discovered that sixty-nine letters and digraphs (pairs of letters that make one sound, such as /ch/ or /ew/) were used to represent thirty-eight sounds in 211 different ways. For example, they found that *oe* was used to represent the different sounds in *shoe, does* (the verb), and *doe* (the deer). Those are a lot of different and conflicting sound-symbol relationships for students to learn! How do they do it?

Why Does Explicit, Systematic Phonics Instruction Work? It May Not Be What You Think!

Systematic phonics instruction makes a bigger contribution to children's growth in reading *words* than alternative programs that provide unsystematic or no phonics instruction (NICHHD 2000a and b). We are not surprised, because children may be learning much more than we are teaching. By systematically drawing students' attention to letters, sounds, and words, we are providing them with opportunities to do what the human brain does best—look for patterns.

Research suggests that the brain is a pattern detector, not a rule applier (Bransford, Brown, and Cocking 1999). While we look at individual letters, we are considering all the familiar letter patterns we know. When the brain finds a word it cannot immediately recognize, it searches its storehouse of known words to find familiar patterns that can be used to figure out the new word (Adams 1990; Cunningham 1995; Fox 2000). For example, even though you probably do not have the word *circumoesophageal* in your regular oral or reading vocabulary, we predict that you can very quickly and accurately pronounce it. That's because you quickly recognize parts of the word by referencing other words you might know—*circum* (circumference), *esopha* (esophagus), *geal* (seal). And you can draw on this same bank of familiar word parts to write unfamiliar words.

Support for this hypothesis also comes from reading research. Tunmer and Nesdale (1985) found that instruction in letter-phoneme correspondences made very little difference in how well children could sound out letter combinations in made-up words (e.g., *flib* and *chate*). However, they did find that the number of real words that children could read did make a difference. The more real words children already knew how to read, the more knowledge they had about the pronunciation of predictable letter patterns, and consequently, the more made-up words they could sound out. Apparently, if you know how to read *fly* and *bib,* then reading the unknown word, *flib,* is easier than if you have to figure out the strange word letter-sound by letter-sound.

It's a Matter of Memory

Barbara Fox (2000), another reading researcher, explained why using "chunks" to figure out unknown words is easier than sounding out individual letters. As you read, all the words first pass through short-term memory on their way to long-term memory. While long-term memory is very large, holding all that you learn throughout a lifetime, short-term memory is extremely limited. Short-term memory can hold only seven thought units, plus or minus two (Miller 1956). And young children's short-term memory is even more limited (Wood 1996). In terms of reading, a thought unit can be an individual letter, a word part, a whole word, or even a whole phrase. A bottleneck occurs when there are so many thought units in short-term memory that some are forgotten before they can be sent to long-term memory. So, sounding out even a four-letter word may present a challenge for young, inexperienced readers; they find it very difficult to hold sounds in short-term memory long enough to figure out a word. But, young children who already recognize some word chunks have less to remember in short-term memory; they put less mental attention and less mental energy into word identification, and consequently, are more successful figuring out new words.

Using the Known to Get to the Unknown

Ursha Goswami (1986) demonstrated that even young and inexperienced readers were able to make analogies between known and unknown print words when the words shared common letters in the same sequence, such as *hark* and *park*. She also found that children were better at making analogies between word parts that form rimes, such as *eat* at the end of *meat,* than they were when the similar letter sequences were at the beginning of words, such as *meat* and *mean.*

Moustafa (1997) did a study of first graders in which she asked, "What better explains children's pronunciation of unfamiliar print words, their knowledge of letter-phoneme correspondences or their knowledge of other print words?" (p. 46). She found that the children's knowledge of common, high-frequency words (e.g., *big, blue, little, old, pretty*) accounted for 95 percent of the unusual words they say correctly. For example, if the children could pronounce *rue,* an unfamiliar word, they almost always could pronounce both *red* and *blue.* Conversely, children's knowledge of letter-phoneme correspondences accounted for only 64 percent of the unfamiliar words they were able to pronounce.

In summary, it may be that systematic phonics instruction is important because it draws attention to letters and sounds, but the children are really noticing letter patterns that are highly predictable. Rimes are parts of words that have stable and predictable pronunciations, such as *ain, ate,* and *an,* as opposed to individual letters that may have many pronunciations.

Now, we turn to spelling research for clues about how children typically develop knowledge of the English orthographic system. This may be helpful in identifying a phonics curriculum based on children's actual development.

Development of Spelling Knowledge

Years of research on spelling development suggests that learners typically progress from a reliance on using sounds of letters to more pattern-based strategies as they gain experience with print and the English spelling system (Beers 1980; Beers and Henderson 1977; Gentry 1980; Henderson, Estes, and Stonecase 1972; Read 1971). Later research with older students led to refinements in the theory of spelling development and suggested a final phase when students learn to make meaning-spelling connections (Bear, Truex, and Barone 1989; Schlagal 1989; Templeton 1983). Although English is a highly complex system that has evolved over thousands of years, it is far more regular than you might expect. However, rather than reflecting a simple relationship of one letter equals one sound, the English spelling system is a complex interrelationship of sound, letter patterns, and meaning relationships.

Henderson (1990) outlines a model of developmental spelling that encompasses the preschool years through adulthood. He divides development into five phases, each with a name to describe students' spelling behavior at that particular time. The phases of development and the learning foci of typical students in those phases provide a useful "curriculum" grounded in how children actually develop. Table 1.1 provides

Table 1.1 Stages of Spelling Development

Stage	Name	Developmental Characteristics
Stage I	Prephonemic	Not yet reading; writing characterized by scribbles or random marks; no relationship between letters used and sounds they make (e.g., *PNoB* for *run*); typical of students in preschool and kindergarten
Stage II	Letter-Name	Letter names used as clues to spelling (e.g., *U* for *you*); most dominant consonant represented (e.g., *SP* for *stop*); typical of students in kindergarten and 1st grade
Stage III	Within-Word-Pattern	Uses consonants and blends correctly; uses CVC and CVCe patterns as clues for spelling, but not always correctly (e.g., *nite* for *night*); typical of students in 1st and 2nd grades
Stage IV	Syllable-Juncture	Most single-syllable words spelled correctly; have difficulty spelling polysyllabic words and applying concepts such as doubling consonants and adding affixes; typical of students in 2nd through 4th grades
Stage V	Derivational-Constancy	Proficient readers and writers who need to learn about the use of Latin and Greek roots and the spelling-meaning connection; typical of students in upper elementary and beyond

a very cursory coverage of the developmental stages and typical learning foci for each stage. We strongly urge you to explore work by Ganske (2000) and Bear, Invernizzi, Templeton, and Johnston (2000) for a more thorough discussion of this developmental theory.

We suggest that the stages of spelling development and the learning foci of each stage provide a useful "curriculum" for assessing student learning and for planning instruction. More information about the specific phonics concepts that are the foci for each stage is presented in Chapter 2.

The Role of Curriculum, Assessment, and Instruction in Designing a Systematic Phonics Program

It is important to remember that phonics instruction needs to be tailored to the developing understandings of the learners. The question for teachers in early literacy contexts is: *How can I teach phonics in a way that is explicit and systematic, based on the student's development, and still use literature, big books, leveled text, writing process, and content area studies as the core of the early literacy program? The answer is to align curriculum, assessment, and instruction to meet the needs of the developing readers.*

Curriculum guides you in choosing letters, sounds, and words to teach. It also provides a general framework for the developmental stages of phonics acquisition. *Assessment* tells you which students know what aspects of the phonics curriculum. Knowing what to teach and to whom, you can systematically plan *instruction* to build on what students know and to teach what students don't yet know.

Figure 1.1 shows a Venn diagram with three overlapping circles. One circle represents curriculum, one represents assessment, and the third represents instruction. Effective teaching and learning occur in the area of the overlap. Effective teaching and learning can occur only when what is taught (curriculum) matches what the learners need (determined through assessment), and when how it is taught (instruction) matches the learners' development and the content to be taught. These three key ingredients of teaching—curriculum, assessment, and instruction—form the organizational structure for the remainder of this book. In Chapter 2 we explore the phonics curriculum using the spelling research on how children typically develop orthographic concepts. Chapters 3, 4, and 5 outline a system for assessing and recording students' learning along the developmental continuum in phonics and spelling. Finally, in Chapters 6 through 10 we look more closely at phonics instruction in preschool, kindergarten, and first and second grades.

Figure 1.1 Matching Curriculum, Assessment, and Instruction for Effective Teaching and Learning

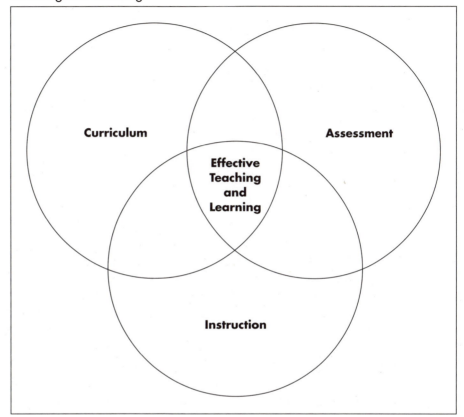

Chapter 2

A Developmental Perspective on Phonics Curriculum

What a sequenced curriculum ignores is the deeper and broader orchestration of "knowing about print" that is being constructed by any single learner.

(Clay 1998, p. 133)

Researchers who have studied young children's literacy development (e.g., Clay 1991; Ehri and Wilce 1985; Ferreiro and Teberosky 1982; Henderson 1984; Holdaway 1979; Read 1975; Strickland and Morrow 1989; Teale and Sulzby 1986) have identified broad categories, or phases, that predict observable changes over time in children's reading and writing. These developmental phases are useful in tracking children's achievement over time and for guiding curriculum planning and instruction. In this chapter we outline the phases in reading and spelling development and work from the spelling research to outline a developmental phonics curriculum to guide phonics instruction in both reading and writing.

A Note About Reliance on Stages of Development

Attempts to neatly tuck young students into either reading or spelling developmental phases is sketchy at best; most students tend to demonstrate characteristics of several categories at once. They are changing quickly and in ways that make it hard to keep up with their curriculum needs. Therefore, categories for reading and spelling development provide only rough guidance for curriculum planning and instruction. Thorough analysis of student reading and writing assessments, as suggested in Chapters 3 and 4, are imperative to match instruction to specific student needs.

Developmental Reading Stages

The stages in reading development are commonly referred to as *emergent, early,* and *transitional* (e.g., Dorn, French, and Jones 1998; Dorn and Soffos 2001; Fountas and Pinnell 1996 and 1999; Mooney 1990; New Zealand Ministry of Education 1994; Parkes 2000). A fourth phase in reading development, the *fluent* phase, is also identified in the literature. Readers in that phase are typically in upper elementary school, middle school, and beyond. Because this book is about teaching phonics in the primary school, we do not discuss implications for phonics instruction of students in the fluent phase. In the following paragraphs we describe the *emergent, early,* and *transitional* phases of reading development in general and use Dorn and Soffos's (2001) suggestions for approximate text levels typically read by children in each stage of development. As either a letter or number system is used frequently to denote changes in text complexity in K–2 books, we include both when referring to text levels.

Emergent Readers

Emergent readers are just what the word *emergent* suggests—they are "emerging." They are beginning to use book reading behaviors, such as moving left to right across text and pointing to words as they say them. They are also learning what words are, how words are different from letters, and how letters differ from each other. Typically, emergent reading begins toward the middle and end of kindergarten. Although, it is also typical to find preschoolers or first graders who are "emerging." Emergent readers can read books at levels A (1) that have highly predictable text structure (e.g., I can run. I can jump.) with pictures that provide strong clues to the text.

Emergent readers have developed phonological and phonemic awareness, and they are ready to move into early phonics instruction. In general, phonics lessons for emergent readers capitalize on children's development in noticing letters and their features, distinguishing between letters and words, and a focus on words and letter sounds that can be associated with the letters in the children's names and common words in the environment.

Early Readers

Early readers recognize and read some words by sight, and they know many letter sounds. In addition, early readers have strategies to monitor and self-correct reading errors; they are able to notice letter clusters (e.g., *th, or*) and word parts (e.g., *ate, ing, ig*) that they can use to help them figure out unknown words. Typically, beginning and mid-year first graders fall in the early reader category. They read texts at levels B (2) through D (5/6) at the beginning of the year and levels E (7/8) through G (11/12) by mid-year. Phonics lessons for early readers may focus on vowel patterns (e.g., *ir, ay, oy*) or learning about words with more complex consonant patterns (e.g., *throb, shrink, belch*). Because the brain is most efficient when it can use patterns to decode words, effective phonics instruction for early readers emphasizes using analogy to known words as a strategy for decoding unknown words.

Transitional Readers

We define transitional readers as those who have developed sight word vocabularies that enable them to read without the support of patterned or familiar text. When they encounter unfamiliar words, they are able to quickly recognize chunks of words and reason by analogy to known words and word parts. Their reading is faster with more automatic problem solving, and reading out loud changes to silent reading. With increased reading rate and efficiency in problem solving, transitional readers can sustain attention to meaning over longer stretches of text, such as chapter books. Typically, students at the end of first grade and throughout second grade are transitional readers. They read text levels H or I (13/14 or 15/16) at the end of first grade, levels J or K (18/20 or 22) at the beginning of second grade, and levels L to M (24 to 28) by the end of second grade.

Transitional readers know quite a bit about solving words, but they benefit from instruction in more complex orthographic concepts for use in reading and writing. Examples of phonics concepts for transitional readers include doubling the final consonant or dropping the *e* before adding endings, common vowel patterns in stressed and unstressed syllables (e.g., *pirate, cartoon, miser*), and common prefixes and suffixes (e.g., *un-, dis-, -ly*).

Connections Between Reading Words and Spelling Words

Early writing experiences support and extend phonics concepts for reading. "Beginning reading and writing share common ground irrespective of the teaching approach used in schools" (Clay 2001, p. 11). Through early writing, young children are learning

- about the features of letters.
- how words are constructed, letter by letter.

- how spaces divide words.
- how print works in a prescribed sequence, left to right and top to bottom.
- how to segment sounds in words (phonemic awareness) they want to write to match them with letters (phonics).
- processes for monitoring and checking on oneself.

Our experiences in classrooms convinced us that early reading and writing experiences have a reciprocal relationship; learning in one area reinforces learning in another. And, it makes sense that it should, because reading and writing share a root: English orthography. Children use their knowledge about how printed words map to sounds to decode (sound out) in reading and to encode (hear and record sounds) in writing.

Developmental Spelling Stages Related to Reading Development

In Chapter 1 we cited Henderson's (1990) developmental model of spelling. The stages Henderson outlines fit nicely with developmental reading stages. Emergent readers are emergent spellers who gradually move from prephonemic spelling strategies into the letter-name stage (i.e., using letter names as clues to spelling words) as they learn letters and letter sounds.

Early readers move quickly from being letter-name spellers, using just the sounds of the letters as clues, to spellers who use letter patterns to spell (i.e., within-word-pattern spelling stage). As they read more complex text that contains words with more complex orthography, early readers use their knowledge of word patterns to figure out new words in reading and writing.

Transitional readers typically change over time from the within-word-pattern stage to the syllable-juncture stage. By the end of second grade typical readers/spellers can read and spell most single-syllable words without difficulty. They are learning how to use their knowledge of patterns on polysyllabic words. They are also learning to use ortho-graphic conventions, such as doubled consonants and common affixes, to read and write new words.

Figure 2.1 summarizes the overlap in reading and spelling stages. Again, we include only those reading and spelling stages typical of students in kindergarten through grade 2.

What's an Affricate Anyway?

Why do you need to know some linguistic details to teach phonics? Knowing something about linguistics—the formal study of language and

Figure 2.1 Overlap of Reading and Spelling Stages

Reading Stage	Developmental Spelling Stage			
	Prephonemic	Letter-Name	Within-Word-Pattern	Syllable-Juncture
Emergent	X ——————— X			
Early		X ——————— X		
Transitional			X ——————— X	

how it works—increases your sophistication in looking at children's language use. For example, if a child writes *jagn* for *dragon,* you won't panic and wonder what's wrong with your phonics instruction. You know that a substitution of /j/ for /dr/ is a reasonable guess for a young student who does not yet know about consonant blends. The sounds /j/ and /dr/ are both affricate and are pronounced with similar mouth positions. If you know that young children in the letter-name stage make spelling decisions based on letter sounds, substituting /j/ for /dr/ is developmentally predictable and appropriate. The error can be explained by development and provides an opportunity for explicit teaching. Although you don't have to be a linguist to teach phonics, it is impossible to talk about phonics without reference to linguistic concepts.

Figure 2.2 is a chart of the linguistic concepts for instruction in grades K–3. This chart can serve as a reference as we explore how these concepts can be taught in later chapters of the book. In Appendix A there is a more complete curriculum outlined by grade and developmental levels.

Learning to Look as Well Hear

With all the emphasis on phonemic awareness it is important to remember that reading and writing require *looking* as well as hearing sounds. Therefore, we want to emphasize the importance of helping children build a strong foundation of letter and sight word knowledge. For decades, letter knowledge was the single greatest predictor of a student's success in learning to read. Knowing letter names is important because it provides a way to talk about printed language, but the ability to visually perceive the features that distinguish one letter from another also contributes to learning to read. *Visual perception of letters is as important to emerging literacy as phonemic awareness.* Preschool teachers can foster the development of visual perception of letters through play such as

Figure 2.2 Linguistic Concepts

Phonological Awareness: An appreciation of the sounds, as well as the meanings, of spoken words.

Phoneme: A single sound in language. For example, *cat* has three phonemes /c/, /a/, and /t/. *Cat* also has three letters, but phonemes and letters do not always match one-to-one.

Phonemic Awareness: The ability to discern phonemes in spoken syllables and words.

Consonants

Consonants: All the letters in the alphabet except *a, e i, o,* and *u. Y* is sometimes a consonant, for example, in *yes, yellow,* and *yokes.*

Consonant Blends: A sequence of two or three consonants, each of which is heard. Examples of initial, or beginning-of-the-word, blends are *st* in *step, cl* in *clam,* and *str* in *strap.* Examples of final consonant blends include *ft* in *lift, mp* in *jump,* and *st* in *best.*

Triple Consonant Blends: Blends of three consonants are a little harder to hear or sound out. They include such triple blends as *squ* in *squeal, scr* in *scrap, spr* in *spring, thr* in *throw, tch* in *ditch,* and *lch* in *belch.*

Consonant Digraphs: Two consonants that together make one phoneme or sound. Consonant digraphs include /sh/, /th/, /ch/, and /wh/.

Hard and Soft c and g: Some consonants can make more than one sound. *c* and *g* are two of them. The "soft" sounds of *c* (/s/) and *g* (/j/) occur when these consonants are followed by *e, i,* or *y* (e.g., *face, city,* and *cage*). The "hard" sounds (/k/ and /g/, respectively) usually occur when *a, u,* or *o* follow the *c* or *g* (e.g., *cut, got,* and *cane*). There are exceptions, however, as in *get* and *give.*

Silent Consonants: Consonants that make no sound in a word. Examples are *k* in *know, w* in *wrong, b* in *comb.*

Vowels

Vowels: a, e, i, o, and *u* are vowels. Some vowels can make many sounds, which are traditionally classified as short or long sounds.

   Short Vowels: The short sound of a vowel usually occurs in words with vowel-consonant-vowel (VCV) patterns, like *cat, bed, kit, mop,* and *hut.*

   Long Vowels: Long vowels usually occur in two patterns: VCVe (e.g., *cake, cute,* and *kite*) or CVVC (e.g., *bean, rain,* and *meet*). Again, when teaching vowel sounds, it is usually best to approach it with word families. Remember, the human brain looks for patterns, not rules!

   R-Controlled Vowels: An *r* after a vowel changes or controls the vowel's sound, as in *dark, her, bird, corn,* and *burn.*

   Abstract Vowels: Vowels that are not influenced by *r* and are neither long nor short, as in *book* and *boot, about, suit, crow, cow, salt.* Frequently, these vowel patterns are called *vowel digraphs* because two vowels (or a vowel and *w* or *l*) come together to make one sound.

Words

Word Families: Groups of words that share an ending, called a rime. For example, *cat, sat,* and *fat* are a word family because they share the rime *at. Cat, sat,* and *fat* rhyme, because they share a rime.

Figure 2.2 Linguistic Concepts *(continued)*

Phonograms: Rimes (e.g., *at*, *ane*, and *eal*) that are found in word families.

Inflected Endings: Endings added to words to indicate certain grammatical relationships. For example, the inflected ending *s* usually means a word has changed to a plural or possessive case, as in "I have three cats." or "The cat's water needs to be changed." The inflected endings *ed* and *ing* change the tense of verbs.

Inflected Ending ed: The inflected ending *ed* may be pronounced three ways: /id/ in *melted*, /d/ in *banged*, or /t/ in *trapped*.

Doubling Consonants: In general, adding an ending adds a syllable. An ending that begins with a vowel (e.g., *ed*, *ing*, *en*, and *er*) added to a word with a short vowel sound requires doubling the final consonant (e.g., *planner*, *hopped*, and *patting*).

Dropping e: When adding endings that begin with a vowel (e.g., *ed*, *ing*, *en*, and *er*) to a word that ends with *e*, you nearly always "drop" the *e* (e.g., *rake + ed = raked*, *bubble + ing = bubbling*, and *shake + en = shaken*).

Homophones: Words that sound alike, but have different spellings and different meanings (e.g., *their/there*, *hear/here*, and *meat/meet*).

Homographs: Homographs are words that are written the same but are pronounced differently (e.g., *read/read*).

Plurals: Nouns that represent more than one of a countable item.

Possessives: Possessives are nouns and pronouns that end in 's to show ownership, as in *child's* or *children's*.

Contractions: Words made up of two or more words, with some letters removed and an apostrophe inserted (e.g., *I am—I'm* and *of the clock—o'clock*).

Compound Words: Words formed by combining two smaller words (e.g., *nighttime* and *somewhere*). Some compound words are hyphenated (e.g., *forty-five*).

Syllables

Syllable: A word or word part that is pronounced with a single, uninterrupted sound of the voice. All syllables have at least one vowel and are denoted by a "beat" when spoken.

Syllable Juncture: The place in a word where one syllable ends and another begins. The word *remember* has two syllable junctures—*re•mem•ber*—and three beats.

Open and Closed Syllables: Two types of syllables are relevant to students learning to read and write words at this level.

> Open syllables typically end with a long vowel sound (e.g., *spi* in *spi•der*, *re* in *re•cess*, and *ro* in *ro•ping*). The pattern at the syllable juncture for open syllables is usually V•CV (e.g., *pa•per*).

> Closed syllables are usually followed by another consonant, which makes the vowel sound short (e.g., *hin•der*, *bun•dle*, and *can•dy*). The pattern at the syllable juncture for closed syllables is usually VC•CV (e.g., *tem•per*).

Stressed and Unstressed Syllables: Refers to how or which syllable is accented. For example, in *remember*, the middle syllable is stressed—*re•MEM•ber*.

Affixes: Units of meaning that can be added to a base word to create a polysyllabic word (e.g., prefixes and suffixes).

> *Prefixes:* Units added to the front of words, as in *reconsider*.

> *Suffixes:* Units added to the ends of words, as in *mainly*.

sorting letters, making letters in rice or sand, tracing large cutouts of letters, and playing with letters made from a variety of materials (e.g., sandpaper, plastic, and rubber).

In addition, knowing some words that can be written without thinking and knowing some words by sight provide an important phonics foundation. They are a base from which other words can be learned. Learners search for the familiar bits from known words and get to new words by analogy. Clay notes, "By the time the list of core words a child controls grows to about forty, the writer controls most of the letter-sound associations of the language, plus the most frequent and regular spelling correspondences, and will have an exemplar of each in his 'known' vocabulary" (1991, p. 244). The same is true of a reading vocabulary. When children have a foundation of known sight words, they have a repertoire of phonics associations they can call upon to apply to unknown words.

A Developmental Phonics Curriculum

In Table 2.1 we summarize a curriculum to guide phonics instruction at each phase of reading and spelling development. Appendix A provides a detailed curriculum outline by grade level and stage of development. We have suggested the grade level typical for learners in each stage. There is a broad linear progression from simple (e.g., letter/sound relationships) to more complex phonics concepts (e.g., syllabification and the spelling/meaning connection); it keeps pace with the gradual progression from simple to more complex texts that the children are reading and writing. The very simplified linear sequence goes something like this:

- Letters, letter sounds, and a few words (emergent)
- Consonant blends/digraphs, CVC and CVCe patterns (early)
- Vowels/vowel digraphs, consonant and vowel patterns in polysyllabic words (transitional)

There isn't a simple one-to-one relationship between a reading stage and a spelling stage. Emerging readers at the preschool level may show only a vague awareness about how writing works by making wavy lines that go left to right or writing random strings of letters (prephonemic stage of spelling). However, emerging readers at the kindergarten level typically move into the letter-name spelling stage as they learn to write their names and the names of their friends and family, and as they participate in instruction that fosters letter and letter/sound knowledge.

Table 2.1 A Developmental Curriculum for Phonics Instruction K–2

Developmental Reading/ Spelling Stage	Grade	Phonics Concepts for Learning/Teaching
Emergent/Prephonemic	Pre-K	Phonological and phonemic awareness and learning about letters through song and a focus on names
Emergent/Letter-Name	K	Still learning letter names and moving to awareness of initial consonant/sound match; learning high frequency words in reading and writing
Early/Letter-Name	1	Final consonants; initial consonant blends and digraphs (e.g., *step, flat, chin, whip*); word families and short vowels (e.g., *dip, sip, lip*); final consonant blends and digraphs (e.g., *bath, hand, song*)
Early/Within-Word-Pattern	1	Long vowels with VCe (e.g., *cane, pine, globe*); r-controlled vowels (e.g., *car, fern, skirt*); common long vowel patterns (e.g., *play, chain, eight*); complex consonant blends (e.g., *throb, shrink, belch, cent, germ*)
Transitional/Within-Word-Pattern	1/2	Vowel digraphs (e.g., *oy/oi, ow/ou, aw*); sounds of patterned inflectional ending (e.g., *lifted, sailed, crushed*); homophones (e.g., *meat/meet, peace/piece, there/their*); contractions (e.g., *they'd, missin', here's*)
Transitional/Syllable-Juncture	2	Compound words (e.g., *bookshelf, headdress, nighttime*); doubling and e-drop with *ed* and *ing* (e.g., *hopping/hoping*); other syllable-juncture doubling (e.g., *paper/butter*); long vowel patterns in the stressed syllable (e.g., *pirate, object, vacant*); r-controlled patterns in the stressed syllable (e.g., *harvest, purple, thirsty*)

The early and transitional stages overlap, or bridge two spelling stages, because there is a wide gamut of text difficulty at each level. For example, the early level bridges simple texts at level B (2) all the way to G (11/12). Children reading text level B (i.e., two lines of text per page and highly predictable structure) are more likely to be ready for phonics concepts in the letter-name stage than the within-word-pattern stage. Conversely, children entering the transitional reading stage at text level H (13/14) are more likely to need phonics concepts at the within-word-pattern stage than transitional readers at the end of grade 2. By the end of grade 2, transitional readers are reading texts at level M (28) and are ready for phonics knowledge related to syllabification.

We want to be clear that the phonics concepts outlined in Table 2.1 are not a linear sequence. The concepts within each stage may be learned or taught in any sequence, dictated by the needs of the learners and the texts they are reading and writing. In addition, students may be moving between two stages; you may need to teach concepts from an earlier stage that a student missed, even though he or she demonstrates use of concepts at a more advanced stage. *But you must not leave the learning to chance.* Some children do learn phonics concepts as though by osmosis through reading and writing. Many children do not, however, and they need explicit, systematic instruction to pick up concepts they missed.

Furthermore, at any grade level you will find a wide range in student development. That's why you will want to do a careful analysis of students' running records of oral reading and writing samples to assess what gaps they may have in phonics understanding. In our developmental phonics curriculum in Table 2.1 the grade level is listed as a benchmark for typical development; it is an indication of what a teacher at that grade level might be teaching if all students were making typical progress.

For a more detailed description of each of these concepts and when to teach them, see Appendix A, Key Concepts to Teach at Different Grade Levels.

The Phonics Curriculum: Concepts, Not Items

The curriculum we propose may not look like a traditional phonics curriculum. Rather than outlining specific items (e.g., the sound of letter *m*), we outline categories of phonics *concepts about how words work* (e.g., initial consonant sounds) that children have to learn. We leave it up to you to choose the particular items from books the children are reading and texts they are writing to illustrate the concepts you want to teach. The texts your students are reading and writing will provide plenty of examples.

Learning and teaching phonics is about learning and teaching how the English orthographic system works. While students do have to learn that the letter *m* makes a particular sound, they also have to learn the much bigger concept that letters go together in particular and principled ways to reliably map onto sounds. This means learning to notice patterns in the orthography—the English spelling system. As you teach phonics, it's helpful to keep asking: What concept for how words work am I teaching here?

How Does This Curriculum Fit with Standards?

National standards for student achievement at the preschool level through third grade are gradually emerging. In the professional literature for teachers you can find consistent and developmentally appropriate recommendations for reading achievement as well as expectations for writing (Dorn, French, and Jones 1998; Dorn and Soffos 2001; Fountas and Pinnell 1996 and 1999; Ganske 2000; Mooney 1990; New Zealand Ministry of Education 1994; Parkes 2000).

Publications by government agencies (Burns, Griffin, and Snow 1999; New Standards Primary Committee 1999; NICHHD 2000a and b; Snow, Burns, and Griffin 1998) report similar expectations for early reading and writing achievement. Because this curriculum is based on recommendations in the current literature for grade-level achievement on text reading and developmental spelling levels, it is right in tune with the emerging national standards for student achievement.

Examples of exactly how to teach phonics in early literacy contexts can be found in Chapters 7 through 10, with each chapter devoted to teaching phonics to students at a particular phase. For now, suffice it to say that phonics can be taught in a variety of ways, and in the context of many activities, in the literacy and content areas. For example, at the kindergarten level you might use the context of shared reading to teach letter names and sounds. Guided reading, interactive writing, learning centers, and content studies also provide contexts for teaching specific phonics concepts to learners at various stages of development. Again, what makes phonics teaching systematic is knowing what to teach, knowing whom to teach it to, having a plan to methodically teach concepts, and keeping records of learning and teaching.

Help! Do My Students Fit the Categories?

Chapters 3 and 4 will give you much more information about how to identify, through assessment, which students need to learn what, because you don't teach a "curriculum," you teach children. However, you can tentatively figure out which category of reader/speller your students fall into if you know their instructional reading levels. Table 2.2 is a rough guide you can use to get started.

In addition, it is safe to say that, in general, you can use your grade level as a guideline, too. In preschool you will probably be teaching phonological and phonemic awareness to most of the class. In kindergarten you will focus most of your instruction on letters, letter sounds, and high-frequency sight words (e.g., *a, the, is, and*). First-graders typically need to learn everything that is outlined for early/letter-name and early/within-word-pattern stages; second-graders usually fall into the transitional/within-word-pattern and syllable-juncture stages.

If your school does not have a systematic plan for phonics instruction, however, you may find students who have large gaps in their

Table 2.2 Instructional Reading Levels and Probable Phonics Categories

Instructional Text Level	Probable Category for Phonics Instruction
Not reading yet	Emergent/Prephonemic
A (1)	Emergent/Letter-Name
B (2)–E (7/8)	Early/Letter-Name
F (9)–G (12)	Early/Within-Word-Pattern
H (13/14–J (18/20)	Transitional/Within-Word-Pattern
K (22)–M (28)	Transitional/Syllable-Juncture Stage

understanding of phonics concepts. In this case, you may need to do much more assessment to find out exactly what students know, and you may need to backtrack to lower developmental levels for instruction.

Another factor to consider in matching students with curriculum is that you have to teach phonics in both reading and writing. In other words, you can't teach a generic phonics lesson based on this curriculum and expect students to automatically transfer the generic concept to their reading and writing. That's what a one-size-fits-all program typically does. Some students make the transfer on their own, but many do not, especially the students who struggle with reading and writing or whose first language isn't English.

Therefore, plan to systematically teach the same phonics concepts in both reading and writing contexts. For example, in kindergarten you might teach letter recognition and letter sounds for reading in a shared reading context. You might teach letter formation and letter sounds for writing in an interactive writing context. Students will quickly understand the rationale for learning letters and sounds if they immediately see how letters and sounds are used to do something they are all eager to do—read and write!

Part 2

Systematic Assessment and Record Keeping

Chapter 3

Phonics Assessments in Reading

The intent behind daily and periodic assessments is to adjust instruction according to student need. The emphasis is on the child, as the teacher determines the timing and sequence of lessons.

(Dahl, Scharer, Lawson, and Grogan 2001, p. 11)

Keeping track of what each student knows and needs to know, and keeping track of what the class as a whole knows and needs to know, are the keys to providing systematic phonics instruction. The only way to avoid the criticism that teaching phonics in the context of reading or writing continuous text is "incidental teaching" is to show that you are systematically recording what students know and then systematically and explicitly teaching what students need to know. In this section on assessment we bring together tools to help you identify what your students know and need to know about phonics.

A good place to begin phonics assessment is by finding each student's instructional text level in reading. In order to read higher and higher text levels, students must learn to decode longer and more complex phonics patterns. Therefore, text level is a tentative guideline for instructing students on phonics concepts outlined in the curriculum in Chapter 2. After you have found the students' instructional text levels using running records, you can analyze the patterns of error and self-correction to home in on exactly which phonics concepts students can use and which ones they need to be taught.

Analyzing Running Records

We recommend the following steps for analysis of running records:

1. Take a running record on a student reading an instructional text. For a kindergartner or first-grader, the text should be one you have read with the student recently in guided reading. For more experienced readers in first and second grades, a new text at the anticipated instructional level will work.
2. Calculate the accuracy rate to ensure the text is read with 90 percent or better accuracy.
3. Categorize errors referring to the stages in the developmental phonics curriculum outlined in Chapter 2, Table 2.1. Appendix B contains forms to help you do this.
4. Focus on errors that indicate a gap in learning from an earlier phase of development or on errors that provide new areas for instruction at the student's predicted level of phonics development. Ignore errors related to phonics concepts taught at higher developmental levels. There should not be many of these; if there are, the text was too hard.
5. Develop a plan for instruction of phonics in reading based on your analysis of running record errors.

Finding Instructional Text Level

A running record of oral reading is a tool to assess students' precise reading behaviors. See Clay's *An Observation Survey of Early Literacy Achievement* (1993) or *Running Records for Classroom Teachers* (2000) for a thorough description of how to take running records. A student's instructional text level in reading is the *highest* text level he or she can read with about 90 percent or better accuracy (Clay 1993). That means a student makes no more than one error for every ten words, for an error ratio of 1:10. If a student makes more than one error for every ten words, then the text is too difficult and the student cannot maintain meaning or learn from instruction.

Finding an Accuracy Rate

To determine a student's error ratio simply divide the number of words the student read by the number of errors, not counting errors that were self-corrected. For example, if a student read 79 words and made 4 errors (79 ÷ 4 = 19.75), the error ratio was 1:19.75 words. This is about 95 percent accuracy. A student who read 79 words and made 11 errors (79 ÷ 11 = 7.18) had an error ratio of 1:7. This is only about 86 percent accuracy.

Analyzing Errors for Phonics Instruction

Students' errors in reading provide windows into their understandings of how to use meaning, language structure, and phonics to make sense of continuous text. For example, an emerging reader who reads *bunny* for *rabbit* is making sense from the text, but she is not using phonics yet. On the other hand, a student who reads *horse* for *house* is using some phonics, but he is not making sense from the text. A student who reads *stopped* for *stayed* in a sentence about a little car that could not go any further and just *stayed* in the middle of the road, is making sense and using some phonics, even if he still made an error. So, running records are a tool to analyze how students use letter and letter cluster sounds (phonics) to read unknown words.

We suggest that a running record assessment of phonics be taken on books that kindergarten and first-grade students have read at least once in a guided reading group. Books that are unfamiliar or too hard will give a skewed view of how young students are using phonics and other sources of information. Once students become transitional readers with much more reading experience under their belts, unfamiliar texts at their instructional level may be used for running records assessments of phonics. Running records can be used to assess students at all levels of reading development.

Analyzing Errors in Running Records to Guide Instruction

There are many instructional directions in which you could go when using students' errors on running records. Of course, you will want to choose instruction that best fits a student's overall level of phonics development. Remember that you are teaching principles for how words work. This is different from teaching to an error just so the student can get the word right. It's a little like the fish parable. You want to teach the students "how to fish" so they can make independent phonics decisions in the future, rather than getting a fish for that day—getting the word right at that one point in time. Knowing how to "fish" to unlock unknown words using phonics makes students independent readers.

Here are some general principles for using students' errors in running records to guide your teaching of phonics concepts:

- Categorize the errors. To categorize an error, use the word in the text rather than the student's substitution, as your frame of reference. For example, if the student reads *kit* for *kite,* the error is on long vowel patterns because the student did not recognize the VCe pattern in *kite*. In general, a quick way to categorize errors is to remember that

- letter-name errors are mostly about consonants.
- within-word-pattern errors are about vowel patterns.
- syllable-juncture errors are about polysyllabic words.

But keep the curriculum in Table 2.1 handy, because there are other concepts at each stage to think about as well. If an error does not seem to fit any category, just call it "other." Look for patterns in the errors that fit within the curriculum guidelines for each stage of development. Again, the forms in Appendix B will help to keep you on track by reminding you of all the concepts at each stage of development.

- Look for errors that are indicative of the student's estimated level of development. For groups of students who make similar errors, plan phonics lessons that teach concepts *within* the students' current estimated level of development.
- Look for errors that reveal gaps in understanding from a previous stage. Teach to close those gaps either by grouping students with similar gaps for small-group instruction or by addressing the gaps in individual instruction.
- Ignore errors that are typically studied at more advanced stages. Simply praise the student for using what he knew to attempt the word, and tell him the word.
- Record as "other" errors that do not seem to fit into any category.

One First-Grade Student's Phonics Development

The following analysis of four running records reflects a student's reading development over time, from the beginning of first grade through the fourth month of school. It tracks a typically progressing first-grader as he moves from the emergent/letter-name stage into the early/letter-name stage and finally into the early/within-word-pattern stage. We include these to show that there is typical progression in development *within* one stage as well as *between* stages, and achievement can be tracked within a stage. Progress is noted as the student grasps more complex concepts within the phase. Although this example is of a student progressing within the letter-name stage before moving to the within-word-pattern stage, similar subtle progressions can be noted in the other stages as well.

September

In September Adam read a level B (2) text, *My Home* (Melser 1981); it shows various animals in their homes until a dog notices a rabbit digging in the vegetable patch. The dog chases the rabbit, who runs quickly into its home in the ground.

Adam read the text quickly with good expression and 89 percent accuracy. He corrected only one of every six errors. Adam paid very little attention to phonics. He looked at the pictures and remembered the story line introduced by his teacher.

- Categories of errors:

    - Letter-name: <u>duck</u>   <u>bunny</u>
                     bird   rabbit
    Whole sentence invented to make sense with story but did not match text: <u>I</u>   <u>like</u>   <u>my</u> <u>home.</u>
                     My   home   is   here.
    - Within-word-pattern: None
    - Syllable-juncture: None

- Within-stage errors: All of Adam's errors are typical of emerging readers who know how to use the meaning and language structure to "read" but are not yet using phonics.
- Gaps in previous-stage learning: None
- Errors beyond estimated developmental level: None
- Other: None

Possible instructional moves: Adam needs to learn how to use the initial letter sound of a word as a cue for monitoring reading and self-correcting errors. An effective prompt at an error is, "That makes sense, but it doesn't look right. Check the first letter." Adam may also need explicit instruction in letter sounds through shared reading and interactive writing activities.

October

By October Adam was reading text level C (3/4). Level C text is much longer, and Adam could no longer rely on his memory for the story or the predictable pattern. *Baby Lamb's First Drink* (Randell 1993) tells the classic tale of a young lamb's birth in the spring and call to be fed.

Adam read this text with 92 percent accuracy, but still self-corrected only one error in six. Now, his reading was more word by word, suggesting he was trying to look at the words for clues.

- Categories of errors:

- Letter-name: <u>thirsty,</u>   <u>Baby,</u>   <u>Mom</u>   <u>my</u>
                     hungry   Baa-Baa   Mother   Baby
- Within-word-pattern: None
- Syllable-juncture: None

- Within-stage errors: All errors are typical of emerging readers at the letter-name stage.
- Gaps in previous-stage learning: None
- Errors beyond estimated developmental level: None
- Other: None

Possible instructional moves: Adam used the initial letter as a clue on two errors, *Baby* for *Baa-Baa* and *Mom* for *Mother.* But on two other errors, *thirsty* for *hungry* and *my* for *baby,* he neglected the phonics clue and let the story structure and his knowledge of young lamb's needing a drink drive his word choices. Adam needs to know how to consistently use the initial letter as a clue to word choice in integration with meaning and language structure. A good prompt at error might be, "Try that again and make it look right and make sense." He may still need explicit instruction on letter and letter-cluster sounds.

November

In the running record for November, *The Jigaree* (Cowley 1988), Adam has made a major shift in his use of phonics information. The level E (7/8) book tells the story of a space boy and fictional creature, Jigaree. The Jigaree wants badly to play with the boy, but the boy constantly does things that make the Jigaree work hard to keep up. Finally, the poor Jigaree just drops to the ground exhausted. The boy relents and offers to take the Jigaree home with him.

Adam read this text with only 80 percent accuracy and a self-correction rate of only one out of every twenty-nine errors. This was because he consistently left the inflected endings off words (e.g., reading *dance* for *dancing*) without significant disruption to the main idea in the picture and the text. Again, the accuracy rate did not really show how Adam was reading. He read the text with some stretches of phrased, fluent reading of repeated language structures.

- Categories of errors:

- Letter-name: <u>Jigaree/jump</u>   <u>for</u> (3x) <u>Jump</u>   <u>after/sc</u> <u>Jigaree</u>
                      jumping   after   Jumping   here   jumping
         <u>dance</u> (3x) <u>Jigarees</u>   <u>swim</u>   <u>swim</u> (3x) <u>Ride</u> (2x) <u>Jigaree</u>
              dancing   swimming   here   swimming   Riding   Jigarees

<u>rides</u> <u>can/sees</u> <u>skates</u> (2x) <u>climb</u> (2x) <u>Fly</u> (2x) <u>flies</u> <u>jumps</u>
ride   is   skating   climbing   Flying   fly   Jigaree

- Within-word-pattern: None
- Syllable-juncture: None

- Within-stage errors: All errors were typical of readers in the letter-name stage. However, now there was a fairly consistent use of the initial letter sound.
- Gaps in previous-stage learning: None
- Errors beyond estimated developmental level: None
- Other: None

Possible instructional moves: Adam used the initial letter consistently as a clue, but he neglected the final phonics information. It indicated Adam's progress within the stage and carried instructional implications. Adam needed to learn how to look beyond the first letter in the word. Because young children easily learn to recognize inflected endings, this would be a good way to teach Adam how to look for and use phonics information at the ends of words. Then during text reading when he fails to use the final phonics information, prompt him: "It could be _____, but it doesn't look right at the end of the word. What part at the end do you recognize?"

December

By December Adam was reading text level G (11/12). The story, *Mushrooms for Dinner* (Randell 1996b), is about a clever little bear who climbs a tree to see where mushrooms might be growing. He picks them for his family's dinner. Adam read the text with 94 percent accuracy and a 1:4 self-correction rate. He read with phrasing, fluency, and expression. Level G is estimated to mark a move into the within-word-pattern stage. Adam's errors suggest he is moving into this stage.

- Categories of errors:
  - Letter-name: <u>no</u>   <u>up/sc</u>   <u>Here/sc</u>   <u>_____/A</u>
                  one   uphill   He   ring/T
  - Within-word-pattern: <u>My</u> <u>fishing</u>   <u>said/finished</u> <u>climb</u>
                         I'm   finding   find   find
    <u>camed/sc</u> <u>Goad/Get</u> <u>t-h_____</u>
    climbed   Good   three/T
  - Syllable-juncture: <u>bucket</u> <u>lovely</u>   <u>_____/A</u>
                       basket   clever   beautiful/T

- Within-stage errors: Many of Adam's errors were on words with phonics patterns typically studied at the within-word-pattern stage: long vowel patterns (e.g., *find, finding, climb*), abstract vowel patterns (e.g., *good*), complex consonants (e.g., *three*), and contractions.
- Gaps in previous-stage learning: The errors at the letter-name stage indicated Adam was still occasionally using incomplete phonics information; on some errors he was led by meaning and language structure and initial letters. However, not recognizing the pattern *ing* in *ring* may represent a gap in knowledge.
- Errors beyond estimated developmental level: The errors on *basket, clever,* and *beautiful* were probably beyond Adam's development because they are polysyllabic words with patterns studied at the syllable-juncture stage.
- Other: None

Possible instructional moves: The errors on Adam's running record show a student who was in progress from one stage to another. He was now integrating use of meaning, structure, and initial and final phonics information. Adam made repeated attempts on some errors (e.g., *Goad/Get* for *Good*) to reconcile all sources of information. Adam's largest group of errors fell into the within-word-pattern area, and this may indicate he was ready to learn long vowel patterns. However, it would probably be good to teach Adam the *ing* pattern before moving on. We would also be looking closely at other running records to be sure there weren't more gaps in Adam's learning. Delay teaching Adam about concepts at the syllable-juncture stage because he is just moving into the within-word-pattern stage, and there is much for him to learn here.

Running Record Analyses in Second Grade

The following three running records are typical of the range of student achievement at second grade.

Luke

Luke is a typically progressing second-grader. The following is his running record at text level L (24).

Luke read *The Missing Pet* (Mead 1998). The main character in the story, James, returns home to find his pet parrot has escaped outside. He recruits his mother and many friends to help him search for his pet. They find clues to follow the missing parrot to the park. In the park the parrot has found a new friend, another parrot. James returns home with two pets for his cage.

Luke read the book with 97 percent accuracy and a 1:3 self-correction rate. While this put the book in an easy range, Luke's reading was choppy and unphrased. He was working slowly to look closely at many words. This is an example of the accuracy rate not indicating how well the student is actually reading a book. Level L is estimated to place Luke in the transitional/syllable-juncture phase in phonics development.

- Categories of errors:
  - Letter-name: None
  - Within-word-pattern: *R*-controlled <u>further</u>
      farther
    abstract vowel patterns <u>ponted</u> (3x) <u>was</u>
                pointed   saw
    contractions <u>His</u>
         He's
  - Syllable-juncture: closed syllables (VC•CV) <u>Casey</u> (2x) <u>further</u>
                Cassie   farther

- Within-stage errors: Luke's estimated instructional text level of L suggests he is at the syllable-juncture stage for study. The errors of *Casey* for *Cassie* and *further* for *farther* would provide opportunities to explore closed syllable patterns.
- Gaps in previous-stage learning: Luke was not able to rapidly recognize vowel patterns in the within-word-pattern area of study: *r*-controlled (*farther*), abstract vowels (*pointed*), and contractions (He's). Therefore, this would be an area for individual instruction.
- Errors beyond estimated developmental level: None
- Other: None

Possible instructional moves: Given that Luke read this level L text with such close attention to the words, we wonder if he would benefit from more instruction at the within-word-pattern level to foster fluent and automatic recognition of many vowel patterns in words. We would continue having him read books in the K (22) and L (24) range and group him for instruction with students who are exploring phonics for reading at the within-word-pattern stage. Luke's case is a good example of how instructional text level can be only an *estimate* of level for phonics instruction.

Danielle

Danielle is a lower-than-expected second-grader. The following is her running record at level G (11/12).

She read *One Sock, Two Socks* (Owens 1992). It is the story of a young boy rushing to get dressed to get to school on time. He can't find two matching socks. His mother is also rushing to get ready for work, and she tries to hurry him along. The charming and supportive pictures show an increasingly frantic mother and child rushing around looking everywhere for two matching socks. They are almost late for school and work when the child notices he has the two matching socks on the same foot.

Danielle read the book with some phrasing, fluency, and expression on frequently occurring language patterns (e.g., "Tick-Tock, said the clock."), and she achieved a borderline instructional-level accuracy score of 89 percent and 1:4 self-correction rate. However, she used phonics information to get to many words she did not immediately recognize. An instructional text level of G (11/12) suggests that Danielle is ready for phonics study at the within-word-pattern level.

- Categories of errors:

  - Letter-name: <u>Ready,</u> <u>his,</u> <u>mother,</u> <u>said</u>   <u>Mom</u>
        Hurry   said   his   mother   Mother

    <u>p-u-ch</u> (consonant digraph)
    push

  - Within-word-pattern: *R*-controlled vowel <u>here</u>; VCe <u>look</u>
                                        hard   like

    and sounds for *ed* <u>t-er-trit</u>, <u>put</u>
                        tried   pulled

  - Syllable-juncture: None

- Within-stage errors: Many of the errors fall within Danielle's estimated level of within-word-pattern.
- Gaps in previous-stage learning: Many of Danielle's errors at the letter-name stage were a case of her being led strongly by the meaning of the story and are probably not really gaps in knowledge. The error of *p-u-ch* for push is an indication that Danielle may need a review of consonant digraphs.
- Errors beyond estimated developmental level: None
- Other: None

Possible instructional moves: These errors suggest Danielle was neglecting even the initial consonants. The *look* for *like* error could indicate a need for more practice with high-frequency words typically studied by students in this stage of development. This running record analysis backs up the estimated level for phonics instruction. We would review consonant digraphs with Danielle in an individual lesson and then group her for phonics instruction with students who are learning to use within-word patterns to figure out words in reading. We would make careful records to ensure we were systematically introducing concepts at this phase of phonics work to be certain that the students in this small group are being introduced to all the within-word patterns for study.

Matthew

Matthew is a second-grader who is typical of advanced transitional readers. Here is his running record at level M.

He read *Crabs, Shrimps, and Lobsters* (Swartz 1997). It is a nonfiction text estimated to be at level M (28). The book is full of fascinating details about the biology of crabs, shrimp, and lobsters. It contains many polysyllabic words (e.g., *tentacles, scavengers,* and *pincers*), but Matthew read it smoothly, with expression, with 99 percent accuracy and a 1:4 self-correction rate. He made only two errors, both on the same word:

>   proton   proton
> "Their meat is tender and rich in protein. We need protein for our bodies to grow" (p. 23).

He self-corrected one error:

>   have/sc
> "Crabs can   live   to be six years old" (p.11).

These errors and the self-correction indicate Matthew is using almost all of the phonics information. It confirms that Matthew is well on track with phonics learning in reading. In fact, it would be difficult to find a text that Matthew could not read easily without going to books that are considerably beyond the interest and experience of a seven-year-old.

However, there are still some implications for instructing Matthew. While an examination of the meaning units or morphology in the word *protein* would be typical instructional matter for students at the derivational-constancy level (usually students at upper elementary and beyond), Matthew is an advanced reader with an interest in words; he might benefit from an enrichment lesson typically taught to older students.

Protein comes from the Greek word *proteios,* meaning "prime" or "chief." Protein is considered the chief constituent of plant and animal bodies. After an explanation of the Greek root of *protein,* Matthew's teacher might venture into an examination of *pro* (means "before" or "forward") as a meaning unit. An examination of affixes is part of the word study at the syllable-juncture stage, and it bridges the realms of phonics (graphophonic) and morphology (meaning connections).

Other Phonics Assessments in Reading

Periodically assessing students' grasp of phonemic awareness and phonics in more formal ways provides information about students' progress toward key benchmarks. This assessment information can be used to report student progress to parents and administrators and to realign curriculum and instruction with changing student needs. Periodic assessments at the beginning of the school year, mid-year, and end of year are generally sufficient to accomplish both purposes. This will allow a comparison of each child's progress over time against both herself and against the progress of the whole group. In addition, assessments scheduled near the end of each ranking quarter provide up-to-date information for parents.

Assessing Phonemic Awareness

It is a good idea to check on students' phonemic awareness near the end of kindergarten. Phonemic awareness seems to be a necessary underlying ability for successful reading acquisition; therefore, you will want to be sure your students have acquired phonemic awareness before they enter first grade. The Dynamic Assessment of Phonemic Awareness (Spector 1992) offers a child-friendly assessment that allows the teacher to provide differing levels of support with the task to distinguish subtle differences in levels of phonemic sensitivity. Using the assessment over time allows you to mark changes in phonemic awareness, rather than just to mark whether students have phonemic awareness or not. Appendix C contains the directions for administering and scoring the Dynamic Assessment of Phonemic Awareness.

The Dynamic Assessment of Phonemic Awareness task is composed of twelve items: four CV words (i.e., *say, pie, we, tow*), four VC words (i.e., *age, eat, egg, if*), and four CVC words (i.e., *leg, feet, page, rice*). These words were chosen because they are probably familiar to most young children and they include a range of vowel and consonant sounds.

The teacher says each word slowly and prompts the child to say each sound. The teacher gives corrective feedback and increasingly supportive prompts and cues when a child is unable to segment a word correctly. For example, if the child can say just the first sound in a word, the teacher prompts for "what comes next" or tells the child how many sounds there are in all. If the child is unable to say any sound, the teacher models sound segmentation with tokens and boxes and the child is helped to imitate the model. A child is considered successful if he or she responds correctly to any of the prompts (including the three that require imitation only).

The child's phonemic awareness score indicates the degree of independence that the child achieves in performing the segmentation task. Progress toward control of phonemic awareness can be indicated over time by both a score and a description of the child's independence with phoneme segmentation (e.g., with model, with prompts, without prompts). We like this phonemic awareness measure because it allows the teacher to teach the unfamiliar task through feedback. Therefore, the measure clearly distinguishes between children who are simply unfamiliar with the task from children who really lack phoneme segmentation ability.

Assessing Letter Knowledge

A letter-naming task assesses letters students know by name. Knowledge of letter names has long been a predictor of success in learning to read and write (Adams 1990; NICHHD 2000a and b; Snow, Burns, and Griffin 1998). However, it's not actually the letter names that are important in learning to read; it is the ability to visually discriminate between letter features that is important (See Adams 1990 for a summary of this research). An essential part of learning how to read and spell in English involves learning how letters form spelling patterns. It is hard to discriminate between spelling patterns (e.g., between -*ain* and -*air*) if you have difficulty discriminating letter features. That is, if you don't really see the differences among *h, n,* and *r,* letters that share a common visual feature of a stick and a curve, you won't easily learn the difference between *hair* and *rain.* One emerging reader we assessed read the words *Go, go, go* as *Go- go- go- go- go*; he pointed to each comma and also read *go.* To his inexperienced eye, the only distinguishing feature in the word *go* was the curve. A comma is a curve; therefore, it must be *go.*

Knowing letter names and how to form letters is important in early spelling development. Students who don't know letter names cannot use letter names as clues to match letters with sounds to attempt their own spellings, which is the first stage in spelling development. A note of caution, however: This does not suggest that learners must learn all the letters and sounds before being introduced to reading and writing (Clay 1991; Moustafa 1997). There is a reciprocal relationship between learning about letters and sounds and learning to read and write. Students learn a little about letters and sounds to jump-start their reading. Then, in the process of learning about all sources of information to extract meaning from reading or to make meaning in writing, they also learn more about letters, sounds, and words.

There are many letter-naming tools commercially available, but you can easily create an inexpensive assessment tool. Simply write the fifty-two letters, both uppercase and lowercase, on separate index cards using clear, bold lettering. On the back of each card, you can write the letter again so that you know what letter the student is looking at as you "flash" the cards. Alternatively, you can use the computer to print the letters in a booklike script by using a font size and style typical of early, leveled, instructional texts. This may actually be the better alternative, because discriminating and naming letters that look like the letters in the books students are reading gives a more accurate assessment of students' visual discrimination abilities. Shuffle the index cards before assessing the student so the letters are randomly organized in case a student has memorized the letter names in *a-b-c* order.

Take a blank piece of paper and fold it in half lengthwise. Label one column "Letters Known" and a second column "Letters Unknown or Confused." Write the student's name and the date at the top of the paper, and you are ready to go. Simply hold up one card at a time and ask the student to name the letter. Of course, this assessment must be accomplished in a one-on-one setting. Record the student's responses in the appropriate column. To save time, if the student knows quite a few of the letters, you might skip recording the knowns and just record the unknowns or confusions. It's the unknowns and confusions you really need to know because they are the letters you need to teach. Alternatively, if the student knows only a few letter names and the rest are unknown, you might record just the known letters and fill in the unknowns later. Write the total number of letters known and unknown or confused at the tops of the appropriate columns. This is one way to quantify the student's learning of letter names across time and to report progress. For example, you could tell parents at ranking quarters how many more letters the student has learned since the last ranking quarter.

When the student confuses one letter with another (e.g., says *n* for *u*), write the student's response on the top and the actual letter on the bottom, as you did with errors on running records and writing samples. Letter confusions are an indication of student learning needs. For example, confusing letters that have similar visual features (e.g., *i* and *j* share a dot; *k* and *x* share sticks at the side; *p* and *b* share circles and lines in a similar configuration) indicates the student needs more experience sorting letters to learn to visually discriminate among them. If a student confuses *c*, *g*, and *e*, this may indicate she has a hard time auditorily discriminating between the letters.

The letter-name assessment is most appropriate for use with emergent and early readers. Typical students know all the letters by the end of kindergarten or middle of first grade at the latest. Once students know all the letter names and read at the transitional phase of reading, it isn't necessary to assess letter knowledge. Appendix F contains a class record form for recording and seeing at a glance what a group of students knows for letter names and sounds.

Assessing Letter-Sound Knowledge

This task assesses the students' knowledge of the sounds that letters typically make. It is a simple measure of early phonics knowledge for reading. You can use the same letter cards just described in the letter-naming task. Again, divide a plain piece of paper in half; label one side "Letter Sounds Known" and the other side "Letter Sounds Unknown or Confused." As you flash the cards a second time to each student in a one-on-one setting, prompt the student to give you a sound. If she can't give a sound, prompt her to give you a word with the letter in it. Many young learners may not know the isolated sound of a letter, but they may be able to tell you, "That's David's letter. He's my brother." From this primitive base you can begin helping the student build a sound/symbol relationship for *D*. However, there is no need to ask for a word association for a letter if a student can already do the more sophisticated task of isolating a letter sound. It is not uncommon for young students to know the sound of a letter in one of its forms (e.g., uppercase or lowercase), but not in the other form or to have a word association for a letter in just one of its forms.

If the student confuses one letter sound with another, note the confusion in the appropriate column, using the convention of noting the student's response on top and the actual letter sound on the bottom. In addition, in the "Letter Sounds Known" column note any words the student gives you instead of sounds by writing the words on top and the letters on the bottom (e.g., *David/D*). This assessment is most appropriate for emerging and very early readers. Once students are under way with reading at the transitional phase, a decoding task may be a more appropriate measure of phonics knowledge for reading.

Names Test of Decoding

To become proficient readers, students must develop the ability to decode unfamiliar words. A decoding task requires students to read words that are unknown in order to assess their knowledge of phonics applied to read words in isolation. One of the easiest and most valid ways to do this is to ask students to read words that you know they don't know. The tricky part is finding words you are sure the students don't know as sight words.

The Names Test, developed by Cunningham (1990) and enhanced by Duffelmeyer, Kruse, Merkley, and Fyfe (1994), is a test that measures decoding, rather than recognition of sight words. The test consists of thirty-five pairs of first and last names selected to meet four criteria (Duffelmeyer et al. 1994, p. 119):

- They are not some of the most common names.
- They are fully decodable (i.e., they sound the way they are spelled).
- They represent a sampling of the most common phonics elements (e.g., consonant blends, short vowels).
- They represent a balance of shorter and longer names.

The Names Test is administered one-on-one. As the student reads the names aloud, you record a check mark on a scoring sheet above each name read correctly. If words are pronounced incorrectly, you record the phonetic spellings for the mispronunciations (e.g., *Bowster* for *Brewster*) above the name. Later, you analyze the results of the test to create a profile of each student's ability to use phonics generalizations to read unknown words in each of these categories:

- initial consonants
- initial consonant blends
- consonant digraphs
- short vowels
- long vowels
- vowel digraphs
- controlled vowels
- schwa

Figure 3.1 shows the result of a Names Test assessment for Matthew, the student whose development we follow throughout these chapters on assessment. The analysis indicates he can decode most phonics patterns. However, he may benefit from explicit instruction about long vowel patterns CVCe (e.g., *Shane*) and CVVC (e.g., *Joan*) in order to

Figure 3.1 Names Test of Decoding Scoring Sheet

Child's Name: Matthew Teacher's Name: ____________

School: ____________ Grade: ______ Date: ______

1. ✓ ✓ Jay Conway	2. ✓ ✓ Tim Cornell	3. ✓ Hō-key Chuck Hoke	4. ✓ ✓ Yolanda Clark
5. ✓ ✓ Kimberly Blake	6. ✓ ✓ Roberta Slade	7. ✓ ✓ Homer Preston	8. ✓ ✓ Gus Quincy
9. ✓ ✓ Cindy Sampson	10. ✓ ✓ Chester Wright	11. ✓ ✓ Ginger Yale	12. ✓ ✓ Patrick Tweed
13. ✓ ✓ Stanley Shaw	14. ✓ ✓ Wendy Swain	15. ✓ ✓ Glen Spencer	16. ✓ ✓ Fred Sherwood
17. ✓ ✓ Flo Thornton	18. ✓ ✓ Bernard Pendergraph	19. ✓ ✓ Dee Skidmore	20. ✓ ✓ Grace Brewster
21. ✓ ✓ Ned Westmorland	22. ✓ ✓ Ron Smitherman	23. ✓ White-lock Troy Whitlock	24. ✓ ✓ Vance Middleton
25. ✓ ✓ Zane Anderson	26. Shăn ✓ Shane Fletcher	27. ✓ ✓ Floyd Sheldon	28. ✓ ✓ Dean Bateman
29. ✓ ✓ Thelma Rinehart	30. ✓ ✓ Austin Shepherd	31. ✓ ✓ Bertha Dale	32. ✓ ✓ Neal Wade
33. ✓ ✓ Jake Murphy	34. John ✓ Joan Brooks	35. ✓ ✓ Gene Loomis	

FINAL SCORE: 66 /70

(ONE POINT FOR EACH FIRST NAME AND ONE POINT FOR EACH LAST NAME CORRECT)

Duffelmeyer, F. A., A. E. Kruse, D. J. Merkley, and S. A. Fyfe. 1994. "Further Validation and Enhancements of the Names Test." *Reading Teacher* 48: 118–128.

decode more efficiently. Appendix D contains a blank form for recording and analyzing student responses and a scoring matrix for the Names Test.

A decoding task, such as the Names Test, is most appropriate for students in the transitional phase of reading, typically at the end of first grade and into second grade and beyond. By using this test with transitional readers, you can quickly assess gaps in students' understanding about phonics concepts and teach to fill the gap.

Why Assess Phonics in Reading and Writing?

In reading continuous text, children have access to much more than the words on the page. They also use their knowledge of the world, their knowledge of the accumulated meanings in the story or nonfiction passage, and their knowledge of language structure (e.g., what word sounds right in a sentence) to identify unfamiliar words. Therefore, they may be able to "read" complex words without exactly knowing the phonics information.

In writing, however, children have to know exactly how the phonics patterns work in order to write complex words. Unlike for reading, there are no additional sources of information to support writing words. Some children do not fit neatly into one category for phonics instruction, because they can read more complex words than they can write. For this reason it is important to assess students' phonics knowledge in writing as well as reading. In Chapter 4 we explore tools for assessing phonics for writing.

Chapter 4

Phonics Assessments in Writing

As teachers, we must observe the subtle changes that occur as children progress from being less competent to more competent spellers. Children's spelling development moves along a continuum that reflects greater control of the spelling system; they acquire knowledge that is shaped through experience and reflective practice.

(Dorn and Soffos 2001, p. 64)

For spelling, it is safe to assume that most of the students at a particular grade level need to be explicitly taught how to use the phonics concepts outlined in the curriculum in Chapter 2. Any writing system, including our English system, is a centuries-old accumulation of conventions for spelling, punctuating, and formatting print. It would be impossible for an individual to learn all the conventions without specific and explicit instruction. Here we do suggest more of a one-size-fits-all approach to instruction. Your grade level can guide you in planning spelling-phonics lessons in writing.

If your school has not adopted a consistent curriculum for phonics instruction, students may have large gaps in their knowledge of spelling patterns and concepts. To discover gaps in students' abilities to use phonics concepts in spelling, an analysis of students' errors in writing samples provides a useful tool.

In first and second grades, you might want to give a specially designed spelling test that includes words with spelling patterns typical at each stage of development outlined in the curriculum. We give an example of such a test later in the chapter. Along with analysis of errors in writing samples, the special spelling test may help you quickly determine which area of the curriculum you need to focus on for phonics instruction in writing.

Analysis of Writing Samples

An analysis of student writing samples can be made in a way that is similar to analysis of running records of reading. It is a useful assessment tool for almost all teachers. We want to caution that it should not be the only means of assessing students' grasp of or gaps in orthographic knowledge. But the starting point for many teachers is an analysis of students' use of phonics in informal settings.

Systematic assessments of each student's writing provides you with a way to look for patterns of change across a task that is completed independently and not like a typical test. It is useful to examine several writing samples from each student. If you have students write in a journal, write in response to reading, and write in the content areas, you will have three types of writing that may reveal a variety of spelling errors for your analysis.

Some schools use writing sample analyses to report progress on report cards. Other schools select samples to analyze after units of genre study in writer's workshop. Part of teaching systematically is having a systematic plan for analyzing spelling errors in order to match instruction to students and to keep track of progress.

Analyzing Writing Samples Step-by-Step

We recommend the following steps for analysis of writing:

1. Select a draft of student writing before it has been edited.
2. Calculate the percentage of conventional spellings. Compare this percentage to that on writing samples analyzed previously to note changes. Take into consideration whether the content of the writing sample indicates that the child is taking risks in spelling to write a more interesting piece or playing it safe with words already known.
3. Categorize spelling errors referring to the stages in the Developmental Phonics Curriculum outlined in Chapter 2. Appendix E has forms to help you do this.
4. Focus on errors that indicate a gap in learning from an earlier phase of development or on errors that provide new areas for instruction at the student's predicted level of phonics development. Ignore errors that are on phonics concepts taught at higher developmental levels. You'll get to higher-level concepts eventually, if you are following the curriculum and the student is on track with development.
5. Develop a plan for next-steps instruction of phonics in writing based on your analysis of spelling errors.

Analyzing Percentage of Words Spelled Conventionally

Periodically select drafts of student writing before they have been edited. First, note the number of conventionally spelled words compared to unconventional spellings. It is helpful in looking for change over time in students' writing to quantify the ratio of conventional to unconventional spellings. However, you would also want to consider the content matter of the writing sample. A student who has a lower percentage of conventionally spelled words because she is trying to write an interesting piece in a new genre or is explaining her science research in a journal is probably doing better than a student who plays it safe by writing only words she knows she can spell. A certain amount of common sense should guide how much weight you give to spelling accuracy rates.

To calculate percentage of conventional spelling in a writing sample:

- Count all the words in the writing sample, including those in the title.
- Count all the unconventional spellings. Subtract the number of unconventional spellings from the number of words written.
- Divide the figure obtained by subtracting unconventional spellings from total words by the total number of words to determine the percentage of conventional spellings.

In the writing sample in Figure 4.1, Matthew wrote 39 words. Only 5 were spelled unconventionally. Here's how to calculate the percentage of conventional to unconventional spellings as Matthew's teacher did on the first page of the writing sample:

- 39 (total words written) – 5 (errors) = 34.
- 34 ÷ 39 = .871, or 87 percent conventional spelling.
- Only 13 percent of the spellings were unconventional.

The fact that Matthew spelled 87 percent of the words conventionally suggests that he has a great deal of knowledge about spelling, especially considering the sophisticated vocabulary he used. To confirm this, do a qualitative analysis of the spelling. You can look for and document students' control over spelling features such as consonants, vowels, and suffixes.

Analyzing Errors for Phonics Concepts

You can also use the simple technique of analyzing the unconventional spellings to determine specific gaps in students' knowledge of phonics

Figure 4.1 Matthew's Writing Sample

Frogs are anfibeyuns. They can stay under water for over two hours. They can breath under water too. They are cood blooded animals. They can also stick out there tongue and catch a tastey bug.

Insyclowpedeya	anfibeyuns	breath	cood	there
Encyclopedia	amphibians	breathe	cold	their

concepts. For example, to look closely at the unconventional spellings, write them on the writing sample or on a separate piece of paper, putting the student's unconventional attempt on top of a line and the conventional spelling of the word underneath, as you do on running record errors. You can see how Matthew's teacher did this at the end of his writing sample in Figure 4.1:

Insyclowpedeya	anfibeyuns	breath	cood	there
Encyclopedia	amphibians	breathe	cold	their

Appendix E has forms you can use to categorize and analyze students' spelling errors in writing samples.

It would be difficult to discern Matthew's stage of spelling development from this sample. Two of the errors, *cood* (abstract vowel) and *there* (homophone), are typical of students in the within-word-pattern stage. But Mr. Porter, Matthew's teacher, already determined through an informal assessment of spelling stage that Matthew can best benefit from instruction at the syllable-juncture stage. Matthew is at the late transitional stage reading fiction and nonfiction text at level M (28). In continuous text he can easily read all of the words he misspelled. However, writing requires much closer attention to apply phonics concepts. Analyzing errors in writing samples is most useful in picking up spelling-phonics concepts that a student may have missed in earlier instruction.

Matthew's errors on the words *encyclopedia* and *amphibians* could be expected because these words contain morphological (meaning) units (e.g., *amphi* in *amphibian* means "on both sides") studied at the derivational-constancy stage by upper elementary or middle schoolers. It is typical, particularly when writing about content area material, that students encounter and misspell words beyond their developmental spelling level. When drawing instructional implications from errors, we usually suggest you try to home in on errors that are within the student's level of development, rather than teach concepts that are beyond. Sometimes, however, it might be a good idea to teach a concept beyond a group of students' estimated level if it will be useful in work they are undertaking. For example, if Matthew and other students are working on a science unit on amphibians, a phonics lesson on morphemes that help students figure out long, "scientific words" might be useful to them.

General Principles for Analyzing Errors in Writing Samples

To analyze spelling errors, you can use the same general principles you used to analyze running record errors:

1. Categorize the errors.
2. Note the errors that are within, below, or above the students' estimated level of phonics development.
3. Make instructional moves guided by curriculum that is within the student's instructional range.

Here are the general principles applied to analyze Matthew's writing sample:

- Categorize the errors. As a reminder, here's the simple framework for roughly identifying error categories.
  - Letter-name errors are mostly about consonants.
  - Within-word-pattern errors are about vowel patterns.
  - Syllable-juncture errors are about polysyllabic words.
  - Derivational-constancy errors are about analyzing words for Greek and Latin roots and other morphological (i.e., meaning-based as opposed to phonics-based) principles.

  In Matthew's limited sample of 5 errors, 2 fell within the curriculum for derivational constancy, and 3 were within the curriculum area for the within-word-pattern stage, which addresses long vowel patterns (*breath/breathe* and *cood/cold*) and homophones (*there/their*).
- Errors within stage: Matthew's teacher identified that Matthew is actually in the syllable-juncture stage of spelling, and he is systematically using the curriculum to guide his phonics lessons for Matthew and others in that stage. This particular writing sample did not reveal any errors for study within the syllable-juncture stage.
- Gaps in understanding: Possible gaps in Matthew's understandings left over from the within-word-pattern stage included the homophones *there/their* and the long vowel spelling patterns in *cold* and *breathe*.
- Errors beyond the estimated stage of development: *Amphibian* and *encyclopedia* were probably beyond Matthew's stage of spelling development.

Possible instructional moves: These errors reveal Matthew's growing awareness of spelling conventions and a few areas for explicit instruction. In a writing conference Matthew's teacher might review with Matthew the *-old* spelling pattern and help him correct the other words. However, it is likely that many other students in this second grade are still confusing *there* and *their*; therefore, Matthew's teacher might do a class mini-lesson. He could give the students a simple memory device for the use of *there,* the word that indicates a place away from you; *there* contains *here,* the opposite of there. Then he might continue the mini-lesson with other homophones and homographs so that students learn the principle of checking for words that sound the same or look the same but mean something different. That will not only help the students fix a particularly vexing spelling problem with *there/their,* but will also teach for extended learning they can use in the future.

Following are writing samples from kindergarten, first grade, and second grade with our analysis and possible instructional moves based on the general instructional principles just described.

Kindergarten Writing Samples

In the following writing samples from a kindergarten in January we have indicated how the students spaced between the words (or didn't) and how they used uppercase and lowercase letters.

Student 1
I LKTO G SW BOD—I like to go snow boarding.

- 6 (total words written) – 5 (errors) = 1.
- 1 ÷ 6 = .166, or 16%, conventional spelling.

Errors:	LK	G	SW	BOD
	like	go	snow	boarding

Student 2
I WOTTOPLAENTHESN—I want to play in the snow.

- 7 (total words written) – 4 (errors) = 3.
- 3 ÷ 7 = .428, or 43%, conventional spelling.

Errors:	WOT	PLA	EN	SN
	want	play	in	snow

Student 3
IWETTO GO TO GrEmES—I want to go to Grammy's.

- 6 (total words written) – 2 (errors) = 4.
- 4 ÷ 6 = .666, or 67%, conventional spelling.

Errors:	WET	GrEmES
	want	Grammy's

Student 4
(Primitive picture with random letters and letterlike forms.)

- 0% conventional writing. Prephonemic stage, therefore, no letter/sound matches or words known.

Because the samples are so short and so similar, we analyze errors and examine instructional moves for students 1, 2, and 3 as a group. Students 1, 2, and 3 are typical of letter-name spellers. They use the names of letters as clues to sounds in words, they can hear and record at least the first and last sound in all words, and they are even using vowels (but not always the right ones) in appropriate places. In addition, they all appear to know the high-frequency words *I* and *to*. *Go* is probably a word that has been taught and learned by some students in this kindergarten, but Student 2 is still not consistent in using it in writing. These three students are reading books at levels A (1) or B (2), simple predictable text with one or two lines of print and pictures explicitly portraying much of the meaning. They are learning phonics concepts in the emergent/letter-name stage. They are right on track for middle of kindergarten.

Let's go through a decision-making analysis using the general principles to guide instruction.

- Categories of errors: Here's where you have to use common sense in analyzing errors. Although you could categorize many errors as within-word-pattern (e.g., vowel patterns, endings), it is not really appropriate given what you know about the overall development of kindergarten writers. Therefore, all errors would be considered characteristic of the emergent/letter-name stage.
- Within-stage errors: All spelling attempts were characteristic of students who are emergent/letter-name spellers.
- Gaps in previous-stage learning: As a group, these students were still not hearing all the sounds in words and representing them. However, their attempts do not reveal a need for phonemic awareness training.
- Errors beyond estimated developmental level: These students were still learning about letters and letter sounds. They were not ready for exploration of vowel patterns in words; vowel patterns are explored after students have a thorough understanding of consonants and a large repertoire of known words from which they can learn about patterns. *Another good rule of thumb is to teach phonics concepts using words students know.* If students do not know a lot of words, then focus on letters and sounds and learning high-frequency words. It

would be better to teach *like* as a word to learn rather than try to explore *-ike* word patterns.

Possible instructional moves: Continue teaching for high-frequency words; *like* would be a good word to teach because young children use it frequently. Use interactive writing lessons to demonstrate how to say words slowly to hear and record all the sounds in words, thus building on phonemic awareness. Teach for recognition of lowercase letters and formation of lowercase letters through interactive writing, shared reading, and learning centers; lowercase letters are used most in reading texts and are needed for conventional writing.

Student 4 is not typical of the rest of the students in this kindergarten. She is not yet reading text in a conventional sense, or writing her name. However, she follows along enthusiastically during shared reading and makes willing attempts to write. This student is more typical of preschoolers at the emergent/prephonemic stage.

Possible instructional moves: Continue phonemic awareness activities through songs, stories, and poems. Begin exploring letters and letter sounds through activities with the name chart. Teach her to write her first name using a capital letter at the beginning and lowercase letters for the rest. Teach her to name the letters in her name. To continue exploring letters, begin with the letters in her name in both the uppercase and lowercase forms. Provide her with many opportunities to sort and categorize letters of different sizes and textures.

First-Grade Writing Samples

Student 1

I have a <u>mogaTcol</u>   <u>cre</u> and my <u>brthr</u> Ryan he has one <u>to</u> and
       remote control   car   brother   too

<u>Ryans</u> can go <u>fast</u>   <u>then</u> <u>myn</u> <u>Ryans</u> is red and <u>myn</u> is <u>pinkh</u>.
Ryan's   faster   than mine Ryan's   mine   pinkish

- 27 (total words written) – 11 (errors) = 16.
- $16 \div 27 = .592$, or 59%, conventional spelling.

Analysis

- Categories of errors:
  - Letter-name: <u>pinkh</u> (consonant digraph)
          pinkish

- Within-word-pattern: <u>myn</u> (VCe)   <u>cre</u> (*r*-controlled)
               mine   car
  <u>to</u> (homophone)
  too
- Syllable-juncture: <u>fast</u>   <u>brthr</u>   <u>Ryans</u>   <u>mogaTcol</u>
            faster   brother   Ryan's   remote control
- Other: *then/than* (could be taught as a homophone in within-word-pattern)

- Within-stage errors: This student's estimated stage is early/within-word-pattern. Therefore, instruction on the VCe pattern and *r*-controlled vowels would be appropriate. Likewise, instruction in the homophones *to, too,* and *two* would be appropriate.
- Gaps in previous-stage learning: The inability to represent the /sh/ sound at the end of *pinkish* may indicate a gap in knowledge of final digraphs. However, *pinkish* is a two-syllable word and this might have made it difficult for the student to apply digraph knowledge.
- Errors beyond estimated developmental level: All the errors on polysyllabic words are probably beyond this student's level. However, the sound of *er* would be discussed in a lesson on *r*-controlled vowels.

Possible instructional moves: Instructional decision making is never clear-cut. But, in general, it is best to focus on concepts that are within the student's estimated stage of development and clear up potential gaps. Therefore, this student's teacher might help Student 1 hear the digraph /sh/ at the end of *pinkish* and review digraphs in general in an individual conference. Student 1 was probably typical of many students in the class at the within-word-pattern stage so the teacher might address the VCe patterns (e.g., *mine*) and *r*-controlled patterns (e.g., *car*) and homophones *to/too/two* in a group lesson. The teacher would probably want to leave inflected endings (*er*), the *-other* spelling pattern (*brother*), or the convention for possessives (*Ryan's*) for later.

Student 2

Mia has a cat that looks like mine <u>icsapt</u> my cat has a white Spot on
                              except

his <u>bellye</u> <u>hr</u>   <u>cats</u> name is Kittkitty my <u>cats</u> name is tommy <u>an</u> my cat
     belly   her cat's   cat's   and

is <u>oldr</u>   <u>An</u>   <u>digr</u>   <u>then</u> <u>hrs</u> She has <u>tow</u> cats I have 1.
   older and bigger than hers   two

- 43 (total words written) – 12 (errors) = 31.
- 31 ÷ 43 = .72, or 72%, conventional spelling.

Analysis

- Categories of errors:

  - Letter-name: *and* is a high-frequency word learned early in first grade when students are typically at the letter-name stage.
  - Within-word-pattern: <u>hr</u> (*r*-controlled) <u>tow</u> (homophone)
      her   two
  - Syllable-juncture: <u>icsapt</u>   <u>bellye</u>   <u>cat</u>   <u>oldr</u>   <u>digr</u>
      except   belly   cat's older bigger
  - Other: *then/than* (could be taught as a homophone in within-word-pattern)

- Within-stage errors: This student's estimated stage is early/within-word-pattern. Therefore, *r*-controlled vowel patterns (*er/her*) would be appropriate. Likewise, instruction in the homophones *to, too,* and *two* would be appropriate.
- Gaps in previous-stage learning: Not knowing how to spell *and* is a gap in this student's knowledge.
- Errors beyond estimated developmental level: All the errors on polysyllabic words are probably beyond this student's level. However, the sound of *er* would be discussed in a lesson on *r*-controlled vowels.

Possible instructional moves: The teacher might address *r*-controlled vowels and the *-ow* vowel pattern (which might help to make clear why *two* is not spelled *tow*) in group lessons. Since many students were probably using the inflected ending *-er,* the teacher might teach this in a whole-class lesson. In an individual conference the teacher might address the *and* error and praise the student for her attempt at spelling *except.* But, doubling the consonant before adding an ending (*digr/bigger*) and *ex* as a common syllable are concepts for later instruction.

Second-Grade Writing Samples

Student 1
This boy is at the transitional/within-word-pattern and syllable-juncture stages.

The Singing Bone
Once upon a time their lived to boys named Michael and Dakota. They loved diging but one day they doug a very deip hole. and fownd a bone and when they tuched it it laughed. So they chined to make it stop laughing but it did not work they had a hard time with the bone. because it would neve be cawiyoit but one day they bared it back up and they lived happily ever after.

- 76 (total words written) – 11 (errors) = 65.
- 65 ÷ 76 = .855, or 85%, conventional spelling.

Analysis

- Categories of errors:
    - Letter-name: <u>chined</u> (affricate) <u>doug</u>—but this error
                          tried   dug
      may be due to the fact that he was learning more about complex vowel patterns; he may have overgeneralized. For example, *dug* and *touched* have similar sounds. He used the more complex vowel pattern on the simpler word *dug* and the simpler vowel representation on the more complex word *touched* (see next item).
    - Within-word-pattern: <u>their</u> and <u>to</u> (homophones)
                                      there   two
      <u>deip</u> (CVVC) <u>fownd</u> and <u>tuched</u> (abstract vowels)
      deep   found   touched
      <u>cawiyeit</u> (complex consonant and abstract vowel)
      quiet
    - Syllable-juncture: <u>diging</u>   <u>bured</u>
                              digging   buried
    - Other: None

- Within-stage errors: This student's estimated stage is transitional/within-word-pattern. He needs to learn vowel patterns *deep, found, touched* as a guide to spelling and how to use more complex consonant patterns such as in *quiet*. Homophones (*their/there, to/too/two*) are an area for study as well.
- Gaps in previous-stage learning: Using the position of the mouth as a guide to spelling the affricates (*tr, ch, j, dr*) is typical of letter-name spellers. This student may have a gap in hearing and using consonant blends and digraphs.
- Errors beyond estimated developmental level: All the errors on polysyllabic words (*digging, never, buried*) are probably beyond this student's level.

Possible instructional moves: This student is typical of many at his grade level. He has gained control over many single-syllable patterns and is bridging the within-word-pattern and syllable-juncture stage. He will benefit from group lessons that systematically address concepts both at the within-word-pattern stage and from instruction that moves him into the syllable-juncture stage, such as how to double the final consonant when adding an ending (*digging*). In an individual conference, or in a small group if others have this gap, the teacher can address hearing and using consonant blends and digraphs. Also in an individual conference, the teacher can help this student sort out when to use *u* or *ou* to represent the short *u* sound. He can remind the student that *-ug* is a predictable pattern and link *dug* to *hug, bug,* and *lug.*

Student 2

This girl is in the transitional/within-word-pattern stage.

> I have a dog his name is Bareon he is big. He is a golden rutrever. He is goldesh redish. He loves me and I love him. He loves to role in the snow and play fech. He noks my brother down. My brother dosent lick my dog. We call him a muss/mucs (two attempts made on this word) because he is big. He barcks lowd. I love him because he is my dog.

We thought you might like to try analyzing this student's writing sample yourself. You can check your analysis with ours at the end of the chapter. First, find the percentage of conventional spellings in the sample to get a sense of accuracy, and then, follow the pattern of error analysis we established: Categorize the errors with the student's attempt on top and the correctly spelled word on bottom; then note whether the errors fall into within, below, or above stages. This student is estimated to be at the within-word-pattern stage in spelling. Finally, suggest some instructional moves.

Analysis of writing samples is an appropriate assessment for students at all ages. It may confirm your ongoing daily observations of students' work and help you catch areas for phonics instruction where students have gaps. In the following section we describe spelling tests to estimate students' control over develomental spelling concepts.

Tests for Estimating Spelling Development

Traditional spelling tests may or may not give you much new information about students' growing phonics competencies; most spelling tests and programs choose words to test and teach that are based on a frequency principle (i.e., words that occur most frequently in English) rather than phonics principles. To confirm what you are finding out about students' phonics needs in writing samples, you can give a periodic spelling test that is specifically designed to give you information about students' phonics understandings. For emergent and early/letter-name readers, the "Hearing and Recording Task" in *An Observation Survey of Early Literacy Achievement* (Clay 1993) provides reliable information about students' growing ability to match letters with sounds in writing. If this task is given at the beginning, middle, and end of the year, it provides evidence of student change over time on a task that is held constant.

For early/within-word-pattern and transitional readers the Developmental Spelling Inventory (DSI) (Ganske 2000) is a reliable way to mark changes in students' stage of spelling development. The DSI is based on Henderson's (1990) stages of spelling development and, therefore, fits well with the curriculum outlined in Chapter 2. The DSI includes a screening inventory to pinpoint a student's likely stage of development and two feature inventories for each spelling stage to help you identify the specific phonics concepts in that stage for instruction. Again, the advantage of using the DSI is that it reveals changes in student achievement across time on a task that is held constant.

You could also design your own phonics spelling test using the curriculum in Chapter 2 as a guide. We designed the following spelling test with words that sample the phonics elements from the four spelling stages, just as the DSI does. The first five words contain phonics elements from the letter-name stage, the next five words represent the within-word-pattern stage, and so on for a total of twenty words. For each stage we selected words that exemplify orthographic concepts that are learning goals for the stage, as outlined in the curriculum in Chapter 2. Table 4.1 lists the twenty words in their spelling stage categories.

Administer this test to a group as you would any spelling test. For the beginning of first grade you might give students just the letter-name words. Students who can spell four or more words correctly on that list should also be asked to spell words on the within-word-pattern list. At the end of first grade and into second grade, you might want to ask students to try spelling all lists.

The student's predicted stage of spelling development is one level beyond the one at which she can spell at least four words correctly. For example, if a student spelled four words correctly at the letter-name stage but only spelled one word correctly at the within-word-pattern

Table 4.1 Quick Assessment of Predicted Spelling Level

Letter-Name Stage	Within-Word-Pattern Stage	Syllable-Juncture Stage	Derivational-Constancy Stage
1. jet	6. smoke	11. contain	16. moisten
2. dash	7. flaw	12. nightgown	17. congestion
3. trip	8. claim	13. ignore	18. electrician
4. lamp	9. growl	14. smiling	19. gravity
5. shine	10. snitch	15. sponsor	20. abundance

level, then her predicted level of spelling for instruction would be within-word-pattern. If a student spelled fewer than four words correctly at the letter-name stage, then that would be his predicted stage for spelling instruction. Students who can spell several words correctly at two stages might be moving between stages and need more instruction at the lower stage. This informal assessment does not provide absolute proof that a student is at a particular level for spelling instruction; it provides only an estimated level. We offer it as another informal tool you might use to confirm findings from your analysis of writing samples.

Record Keeping: The Other Half of Systematic Assessment

Assessing students' phonics knowledge is only one part of the systematic assessment equation. In order to use assessment to guide instructional decisions, you must have at your finger tips what the students know. In the complex setting of an elementary classroom, with many students at different levels of development and many subjects to teach, keeping accurate records of your assessments is the only way to ensure you can match phonics instruction to students' needs. In Chapter 5 we suggest ways to keep track of student assessment information.

Analysis of the Writing Sample

Compare the analysis you made of student 2's writing sample with our analysis. Remember that student 2 is at the transitional/within-word-pattern stage.

Analysis of a Second-Grade Writing Sample for Student 2

- 68 (total words written) – 11 (errors) = 57.
- 57 ÷ 68 = .838, or 84%, conventional spelling.

Analysis

- Categories of errors:
  - Letter-name: <u>lick</u>—*like* is a high-frequency word
    like
  - Within-word-pattern: <u>role</u> and <u>lick</u> (long vowel patterns)
    roll   like

        noks (silent consonant) fech (complex consonant)
        knocks   fetch
        dosent (contraction) barcks (use of *k* at end)
        doesn't   barks
        lowd and muss/mucs (abstract vowels and soft *c*?)
        loud   moose

- Syllable-juncture: rutrever goldesh redish
                       retriever goldish reddish

- Other: None

- Within-stage errors: This student's estimated stage is transitional/within-word-pattern. She needs to learn many concepts typical of this stage: when to use *ck* or just *k* at the end of a word, silent consonants (*knock*), vowel patterns (**like, moose, loud, bark**), complex consonant patters (*fetch*), and contractions.
- Gaps in previous-stage learning: Not knowing how to spell *like* is a gap in this student's knowledge.
- Errors beyond estimated developmental level: All the errors on polysyllabic words (*retriever, goldish, reddish*) are probably beyond this student's level.

Possible instructional moves: This student is typical of many at her grade level. She will benefit from group lessons that systematically address concepts at the within-word-pattern stage. In an individual conference, the teacher can address the gap in knowing how to spell *like* and extend it to other words with the *–ike* spelling pattern.

Chapter 5

Making It Systematic: Keeping Records

In order to be effective, you need detailed knowledge of the children in your program so you can adjust tasks and materials to help children make the most of their strengths. Through systematic observation, you can collect behavioral evidence of learning.

(Pinnell and Fountas 1998, p. 15)

A systematic phonics program must include a plan for record keeping. You will need a way to record

- your analysis of individual student work, like running records and writing samples, in order to plan instruction.
- reading and spelling levels of your class as a whole in order to group students for instruction.
- individual student achievement over time in order to talk with parents, administrators, or the school literacy team (e.g., classroom teachers, special educators, literacy specialists, Title I tutors) about student progress or lack of progress in phonics.
- what you taught and whom you taught it to so that no students fall between the cracks in phonics instruction.

In this chapter we suggest systems for recording class achievement and individual student achievement, and we suggest ways to keep track of what you have taught and to whom.

Class Achievement Record

Table 5.1 is a class profile for a second grade in the third month of school. The second-grade teacher wanted to see at a glance how all the

Table 5.1 Student Achievement at a Glance

Grade 2, Mr. Porter   November 2001

Student's Name	Reading Text Level	Spelling Stage	Names Test
Toby	E (8)	LN—>WW	6/70
Alex	G (11/12)	LN—>WW	11/70
Danielle	G	LN—>WW	10/70
Spencer	H (13/14)	LN—>WW	12/70
Miranda	H	LN—>WW	9/70
Nathan	H	LN—>WW	12/70
Mia	J (18/20)	WW	21/70
Devon	J	WW	25/70
Keisha	J	WW	20/70
Jeremy	J	WW	18/70
Kate	J	WW	26/70
Michael	K (22)	WW	39/70
Jessica	K	WW	35/70
Sarah	K	WW	40/70
Maria	K	WW	32/70
Darnel	K	WW	29/70
Jerome	K	WW	36/70
Sierra	K	WW	39/70
Melanie	M (28)	SJ	67/70
Matthew	M	SJ	66/70
Caleb	M	WW—>SJ	64/70
Jenna	O (32/34)	SJ	69/70
Darrell	O	SJ	70/70

students were doing. He administered a small number of assessments, including running records, the Names Test, and a quick spelling-stage assessment. He included only levels and scores on this one-page profile so that he could quickly see where students needed to be grouped for instruction. He has more information on each student, such as what specific phonics patterns they can use or need help with, on individual student record forms.

Using a Class Assessment Profile to Plan Instruction

With this class-at-a-glance record you can see that the majority of students are reading between levels J (18) and M (28). This pattern of progress suggests that the majority of students have moved into the transitional phase of reading. A closer examination of errors students make on decoding unfamiliar names on the Names Test indicates the majority make few errors on initial consonants, consonant blends, consonant digraphs, or short vowels. The teacher will probably do most of his phonics instruction for reading in the context of guided reading groups, linking work with the word wall when possible.

Analysis of writing samples and the quick spelling test confirm that many of the students are at the within-word-pattern spelling stage. The teacher will do whole-class mini-lessons during writer's workshop to ensure that he *systematically* covers phonics concepts at the within-word-pattern spelling stage. When he discovers lapses in the use of particular concepts through analysis of individual writing samples, he will address the area in a writing conference or teach the concept in a small group if several students appear to need to learn the concept.

There are students in this second grade who lie outside the typical class performance. Six students are still early readers, reading at levels E (8) and G (11/12). Two students are just entering the transitional phase at level H (13/14). These six students are between the letter-name and the within-word-pattern spelling stages. They still need work on orthographic concepts in the letter-name stage.

In contrast, two children are above the class norm, reading at instructional level O (about text level 30); they are spelling consistently at syllable-juncture stage. Although the class-at-a-glance record is a good way to begin grouping students for instruction, you need much more information at your fingertips to plan specific instruction.

A More In-Depth Class Phonics Profile

Figure 5.1 is an example of a class record form that would contain more in-depth assessment data for this second grade. We have filled in the information for Matthew's assessments that were used throughout Chapters 3 and 4. In the first space in the row we wrote Matthew's name and recorded our anecdotal comment related to his overall reading and writing development.

In the reading section, we recorded Matthew's predicted level for guided reading instruction in the Text Reading box. Even though he read a level M text easily, we think he needs to read more broadly at this level before moving up. We also made a statement that describes how Matthew used meaning, language structure, and phonics on this level M text. For instructional purposes, it's helpful to be as specific as you can about how the student uses phonics information on running records. We recorded that on two errors he had difficulty decoding the -*ein* spelling pattern and gave the exact substitution that led us to this comment.

Figure 5.1 Class Phonics Profile

Grade **2**   Teacher **R. Porter**   Date **Nov. 15, 2001**

Name and Comments	READING		WRITING	
	Text Reading	Names Test	Writing Sample	Predicted Spelling Stage
Name: **Matthew** Comments: *Fluent reader and competent writer*	Level: **M** Use of information: *Integrates all sources of information.* *Needs work on more advanced phonics patterns.* *2x Proten protein*	Score: **66**/70 Work needed on: *• Long vowel patterns with silent e* shan white (shane) whit Hō-key Hoke	% Conventional Spelling **87%** % Unconventional Spelling **13%** Work needed on: *-old, there/their,* *(ph), -ia, -ian* *(Nonfiction)*	Stage: **Syllable Juncture** Work needed on: *• R-controlled vowels* *• Unstressed syllables*
Name: Comments:	Level: _____ Use of information:	Score: _____/70 Work needed on:	% Conventional Spelling _____ % Unconventional Spelling _____ Work needed on:	Stage: _____ Work needed on:
Name: Comments:	Level: _____ Use of information:	Score: _____/70 Work needed on:	% Conventional Spelling _____ % Unconventional Spelling _____ Work needed on:	Stage: _____ Work needed on:

The second box in the reading section contains information on the Names Test. We recorded Matthew's score of 66 correct out of 70 names and our comment about more areas for instruction. We can see a picture emerging of a highly competent second-grader; it suggests that he is at the end of the transitional level in reading and working on concepts in the syllable-juncture stage in spelling.

In the next two spaces we recorded information from the writing assessments. In the writing sample section we noted that on this writing sample he had 87 percent conventional spelling and 13 percent unconventional spelling. We noted he needs to review the *-old* pattern and use of *there/their*. We also noted that he needs work on *ph* and *-ia* and *-ian*. In the box for information from the informal spelling assessment we recorded Matthew's predicted spelling stage and made a note about particular areas for instruction. Again, this presents a consistent picture of a second-grader well on his way in the use of phonics for writing.

This same form could be used by a kindergarten or first-grade teacher, but it would probably not include information from the Names Test. Instead, a kindergarten or first-grade teacher might supplement this form with one that records the students' knowledge of letter names and sounds. Appendix F has a form to record letter and letter-sound knowledge for a class. Appendix F also includes class record forms and individual record forms that you can copy.

Individual Achievement Record

It is important to record a student's changes from one assessment period to another to be sure the student is making the expected progress in learning and using phonics. Following are descriptions of forms to record an individual's phonics assessment results at three points in time across the school year.

Preschool Through First Grade

Figure 5.2 is an individual record of progress in phonics over time for preschool through first-grade students. It shows one student's assessment information over time. The form is divided into three columns, one for beginning-of-year, one for mid-year, and one for end-of-year information. It is a form for recording information on younger students (e.g., preschool to first grade) for whom learning letter names and sounds is still a goal. In each column there is room to record information on letter names, letter sounds, text reading, a writing sample

Figure 5.2 Phonics Development over Time: Individual Record Sheet for Grades Pre-K, K, and 1

Name: _Manuel_
Grade: _K_

	Beginning of Year Date: _August 29_	Mid Year Date: _January 10_	End of Year Date: _June 6_
Letter Names	# Uppercase Known _21_/26 # Lowercase Known _5_/26 Unknown/Confused: F, K, N/Z, J, Q knows lower case: a, x, o, w, s	# Uppercase Known _25_/26 # Lowercase Known _19_/26 Unknown/Confused: U/Q, K/u, P/q, g/e, Y/v, i/l, b/d, h/n	# Uppercase Known _26_/26 # Lowercase Known _24_/26 Unknown/Confused: P/q, #1/l
Letter Sounds	# Uppercase Sounds Known _1_/26 # Lowercase Sounds Known ___/26 Unknown/Confused: knew his name for upper case M	# Uppercase Sounds Known _6_/26 # Lowercase Sounds Known _3_/26 ~~Unknown/Confused:~~ Knows: - F, B, M, D, S and m, k, s	# Uppercase Sounds Known _15_/26 # Lowercase Sounds Known _13_/26 Unknown/~~Confused~~: U/u, C/c, Y/y, Q/q, N/n, X/x, I/i, E/e, G/g, R/r, V/v, a, j
Text Reading	Level: _/_ Use of information: Located own name on name chart	Level: _1_ Use of information: Uses pictures and memory for text. One-to-one match not consistent	Level: _3_ Use of information: Uses pictures, memory for text and some beginning letters. Get like Knows: Go, love, the, is, a, I, me
Writing Sample	% Conventional Spelling ___ % Unconventional Spelling ___ ~~Work needed on:~~ Wrote name in upper case letters on picture	% Conventional Spelling ___ % Unconventional Spelling _100%_ ~~Work needed on:~~ Wrote name in upper + lower case - Attempted a few words: D/dog	% Conventional Spelling _33%_ % Unconventional Spelling _66%_ ~~Work needed on:~~ I PD BSL. played Baseball
Predicted Spelling Stage	Stage: _Prephonemic_ Work needed on: Draws pictures but no attempt at words	Stage: _Early Letter Name_ Work needed on: Records some initial and final letters when encouraged	Stage: _Letter Name_ Work needed on: Records all dominant consonants

analysis, and an informal spelling-stage assessment. It provides a nice record of one student's phonics development over one school year.

At the beginning of the school year Manuel was an emerging reader: He knew some letters and letter sounds, he knew how books worked, and he could write some words that were important to him (e.g., his name, *mom, dad*). He could read a level A (1) text if his teacher read it to him first, but he was only using meaning and language structure as sources of information; he used no letter sounds as cues. His writing was largely unconventional, typical of very young writers in the emergent/prephonemic stage of spelling who use a limited knowledge of letter names to make decisions about spelling words.

However, by the end of the year, Manuel was exhibiting achievement typical of readers entering the early phase: He could read text level C (3/4), using initial letters as cues to unknown words, he knew most of the letters and their sounds, and he could read a few high-frequency words (e.g., *the, is*) in isolation. In writing at the end of the year, he was typical of spellers in the letter-name stage, and he had a greater percentage of conventional words represented in his writing sample. Manuel is on a typical trajectory of progress.

First Through Second Grades

Figure 5.3 is also a form to record one student's progress over a school year, but it is adapted for use with more experienced students in first through second grades who already know letter names and sounds. It provides a space to record information from analysis of running records, the Names Test, a writing sample, and an informal spelling-stage assessment.

Figure 5.3 tells the achievement story about a second-grade student. Danielle began the school year reading text level G (12), several levels below the school benchmark of text level J (18/20) for entering second-graders. By mid-year she was where most second-graders are at the beginning of the year. And by the end of the year, she was only on text level K (22), below the benchmark level of M (28) for the end of grade 2. The teacher's statement about Danielle's use of information on text reading indicates that she is not using all the phonics information to analyze unknown words on text reading. This is corroborated by her performance on the Names Test. This assessment indicates she is still having difficulties with most vowel patterns.

In writing, an informal spelling-stage assessment indicates Danielle is between the letter-name and the within-word-pattern stages of development. She still needs to work on consonant blends and digraphs and CVC pattern words. Her writing sample reveals a very low percentage of

Figure 5.3 Phonics Development over Time: Individual Record Sheet for Grades 1, 2, and 3

Name: _Danielle_

Grade: _2_

	Beginning of Year Date: _September 5_	Mid Year Date: _January 19_	End of Year Date: _June 10_
Text Reading	Level: _12_ Use of information: Uses meaning, language structure and limited letter cues at error	Level: _18_ Use of information: Uses meaning and structure and initial and final visual information	Level: _22_ Use of information: Uses meaning and structure and letter patterns, but process is slow.
Names Test	Score: _2_ / 70 ~~Work needed on:~~ Uses only initial letters as cues; does not know how to analyze unknown words	Score: _7_ / 70 Work needed on: next: consonant blends, long vowels, decoding 2 syllables	Score: _16_ / 70 Work needed on: Digraphs, controlled vowels, using known CVC and CVCe patterns to get to unknown.
Writing Sample	% Conventional Spelling _12%_ % Unconventional Spelling _88%_ Work needed on: High frequency words, letter-sound matches, vowels	% Conventional Spelling _20%_ % Unconventional Spelling _80%_ Work needed on: High frequency words and CVC and CVCe patterns	% Conventional Spelling _50%_ % Unconventional Spelling _50%_ Work needed on: Complex consonants and vowel patterns $\frac{sing}{spring}$, $\frac{fite}{fight}$
Predicted Spelling Stage	Stage: _Letter Name_ Work needed on: CVC patterns, inflected endings	Stage: _Letter Name_ Work needed on: Generating new words from known CVC patterns	Stage: _LN → Within Word_ Work needed on: long vowel patterns

conventional spellings and confirms that she still needs work on all short and long vowel patterns.

Keeping Track of Your Teaching

To keep you on track and ensure that you provide instruction in the key curriculum concepts for phonics outlined in Chapter 2, you need a record that tells you at a glance what the concepts are and when you taught them. Appendix G contains forms you could use to keep track of your instruction. The forms are organized by reading/spelling stage and include all the phonics concepts from the curriculum for that stage.

One form is for recording the specific concepts taught and the date on which the concepts were taught to specific students in shared or guided reading. The other is a form for recording the same information for whole-group phonics lessons in spelling. The forms can be adapted to keep records of phonics instruction for individual students as well. Simply cross out the headings and write in the student's name to indicate this is a record of instruction for this particular student.

Using Student Performance to Assess Curriculum and Instruction

Assessments are not only a measure of a student's or group's progress; they are also a measure of our curriculum and instruction. The young learners and their parents must rely on the opportunities for learning that our curriculum and instruction provide. Therefore, all assessments should also be ways for you to evaluate the success of your curriculum.

For example, the student samples at each grade level used in the section on analyzing errors in writing in Chapter 4 came from the same classrooms. You will notice in the kindergarten samples, except for Student 4, a similar pattern in words spelled correctly and ability to hear and record sounds. We can tell that this teacher is doing a good job of teaching her students letters and sounds and how to use that knowledge to compose a meaningful sentence. We can also tell that she is not systematically teaching the students how to form lowercase letters. We suspect that the kindergarten curriculum is missing a section on lowercase letter formation.

To use student writing to assess your curriculum and instruction, randomly select about five samples from among the whole group for analysis. Note patterns in words spelled correctly and in errors. What have you been teaching and where can you find a gap?

To see what you have and have not been teaching in guided reading groups, take running records on all children in the same group as they reread their newest instructional text. First, check to see if your book selection was appropriate and if the students were grouped effectively by noting the error rate. If the book was appropriate and the grouping was effective, all running records will indicate the book is well within the students' instructional and easy range. Then analyze the accuracy and error patterns and ask yourself the two questions: (1) What have I taught? and (2) Where have I left gaps?

Finding Time for Assessment and Record Keeping

Admittedly, it is much more complex to assess students' needs and match instruction to the students than simply to implement a one-size-fits-all phonics program. However, the classroom reality is that there are many time demands on a teacher with twenty-five to thirty students. To find time for assessment, some schools have developed alternative approaches such as the following:

- Some schools ask parents to bring students in the week before school begins so teachers can schedule one-on-one assessments. They find that most parents are very willing to do this, especially when parents understand the benefit it will have for their children.
- To cope with mid-year and end-of-year assessments, some schools hire substitute teachers who cover classes while the teachers complete one-on-one assessments.
- Other teachers have found it a worthwhile compromise to halt their regular instructional schedule for a week of assessment. Students complete work that reviews or consolidates old learning or engage in self-evaluations (e.g., evaluate one of their writing samples using a simple rubric the class develops together) to contribute to their portfolios while the teachers devote classroom time to one-on-one assessments. It is probably good practice for the regular classroom routine to be halted periodically for everyone to take stock of where they are in their learning and where they need to go.
- Another option in schools where there are paraprofessionals or university interns is to train them to do assessments. For example, a paraprofessional or university student could be trained to administer the letter-name and letter-sound tasks to young children.

There are advantages and disadvantages to all of these assessment options. You need to weigh the alternatives to decide which will suit your school situation. The bottom line is you must find time to assess student development in order to teach efficiently and effectively so that students make steady progress in learning.

If you have a systematic plan for assessing student knowledge of phonics related to the developmental curriculum, and you have a systematic plan for keeping track of what you teach and to whom, you are well on your way to *teaching phonics systematically*. In the remaining chapters we complete the third area to be considered for effective teaching and learning: instruction.

Part 3

Explicit, Systematic Phonics Instruction

Chapter 6

Instructional Methods

Children who read and write texts can get unlimited exposure to learning letters, sounds, and words, and teachers can extract suitable examples from the texts around the classroom at any time in any lesson, at any time of day.

(Clay 2001, p. 94)

Teachers in primary classrooms are afforded many opportunities to teach children phonemic awareness and phonics skills. Calendar activities, class rules, math, science, and social studies provide teachers and children with avenues for use and continued growth in phonemic awareness and phonics. It is, however, necessary for teachers in the primary grades to devote time each day to the specific teaching of phonemic awareness and phonics.

The Literacy Block

The literacy block is an extended period of time set aside each day for the teaching and practice of reading, writing, phonemic awareness, phonics, spelling, and word study. Schools generally allow from one and one-half to two and one-half hours daily for the literacy block. School scheduling does not always allow every grade to have a two and one half hour block of uninterrupted literacy learning. The scheduling of special subjects (art, music, PE, library, computer, etc.) and the necessity of staggered lunch times require teachers and administrators to make careful choices regarding schedules. It is possible, however, for principals and teachers to work together to develop schedules that serve the literacy needs of children. Through careful planning, large uninterrupted blocks of time can be carved out for each class. (Sample class schedules for grades pre-K through 2 are offered in Chapters 7 through 10.)

The literacy block is the ideal place for the instruction and practice of phonics and phonemic awareness lessons. During this block of time teachers and children may engage in read-aloud, shared reading and writing, spelling, word study, guided reading, and writing workshop. In addition, there are opportunities for independent practice. Savvy teachers use this time not only to teach phonemic awareness and phonics, but also to show children why this knowledge is useful.

Shared Reading

While phonics instruction can and should take place throughout the school day, we believe shared reading and writing situations provide ideal contexts for explicit teaching. During shared reading, the children and teacher read an enlarged text (big books or overhead projections) together. The nature of shared reading is one of clear demonstration of the reading process. As the teacher and children read, opportunities to demonstrate how to use phonemic awareness and phonics knowledge occur often in well-planned lessons.

During shared reading, the initial reading of the enlarged text is supported by the teacher. The text is re-read often over a period of days. Children quickly become familiar with the text and are able to follow along with the teacher and their classmates. Throughout the process, the teacher and children hold conversations about the meaning of the book. Additional features and deeper understandings occur with each reading.

Once the children are very familiar with the text, the teacher may use it for the explicit teaching of phonics. The children's familiarity with the text frees them to focus on the particular skill the teacher has decided to teach. For example, a first-grade teacher might write the word *apartment* on a small white board. The children could practice breaking the word into syllables by saying the word aloud and clapping each part. They could then look for parts they know, such as the *ar* or *ment.* With the teacher for support, they could use what they know about letter sounds and phonics rules to figure out the word. The wise teacher asks the children to say what they think the word is, then asks them to put the word back into the text to determine if the word also makes sense. She will remind the children to use this strategy during independent reading.

Shared Writing

Just as shared reading makes the reading process visible to children, shared writing makes the writing process visible. After the children and teacher compose texts, the actual scribing of the text is used to prompt children to use their knowledge of phonemic awareness and phonics. For example, if the children want to write the word *panda* while researching and writing about bears, they could use their knowledge of initial consonant sounds and the *an* chunk to determine the first syllable *pan*. The children could say *panda* slowly and listen to the final syllable. One class was able to hear the *d* but became confused by the sound of *a* at the end of *panda*. The teacher reminded the children of a story the class had read about a pig named Amanda. By connecting the last syllables in the words *Amanda* and *panda,* the children were able to complete the word *panda.* The children were helped to see the connection of this new learning to their own independent writing.

Shared writing allows children to learn about and practice writing their thoughts while enjoying the support of the teacher and their classmates. At times the teacher may do the writing and ask the children to help her decide how to write some of the words. At other times the children write the text with the help of the teacher and their classmates. As the children make decisions, they are encouraged to use the skills they have learned during phonics lessons, word study, and spelling instruction. Again, children see a purpose for this knowledge.

Products from shared writing, and reading materials used for shared reading lessons are accessible to children throughout the day. The familiar texts are used as references for further instruction in phonics. As children grow as readers and writers, the richness and complexity of their shared reading and writing support their learning of increasingly complex phonics rules. It is not necessary for teachers to select books for shared reading to support the specific phonics skill being taught. The phonics skills readers need will appear often in quality reading materials.

Guided Reading and Writing Workshop

Guided reading and writing workshop are places to address the specific needs of individuals and small groups of children with similar needs. Teachers also use this time to assess and look for evidence of independent use of phonics and phonemics awareness strategies. This new information will guide future instruction.

During guided reading, the teacher meets with small, homogeneous groups. The children and teacher spend from fifteen to thirty minutes focused on the specific needs of the group. This means that a typical classroom of twenty children may have as many as four groups. In a first-grade classroom in October, Group 1 needed to effectively learn to use initial and final consonant sounds to decode. Group 2 needed to practice looking for and using initial consonant blends and digraphs. Group 3 was practicing the use of onset and rime, while Group 4 was learning about root words. As each group worked on its specific needs, the teacher offered instruction and support. She also kept careful records of progress.

The first few minutes of writing workshop are spent learning strategies via mini-lessons, based on the needs of the young writers. As young children learn to hear and record sounds in words, mini-lessons during writing workshop may include useful phonemic awareness and phonics strategies to use while writing.

During writing workshop children write, revise, and edit pieces of writing they have composed. While the class is writing, the teacher confers with individual children. Based on the needs of the child, the teacher may use this time to support individual writers' use of phonics strategies. By assisting children in this way, the teacher again is able to help children understand and apply phonics concepts.

Print-Rich Classrooms

In order to build community, most teachers lead children in discussions about appropriate classroom behaviors. Once the group determines the appropriate behaviors, a list is usually written and posted in the room. Other printed materials displayed in classrooms might include class schedules, calendars, morning messages, and word walls. Commercial and student-made alphabet, color, and shape charts can be posted along with interactive and shared writing products. The work of individuals and small groups of students also adorns many classroom walls. This printed material serves as a tool for teaching and learning about phonemic awareness and phonics.

In a print-rich classroom children become familiar with and are able to read a wide variety of materials. These materials are known to the entire class and can be used to reinforce and learn new concepts. For example, teachers often ask children to "read the room," that is, to look for all the words they can find with, for example, the long *a* sound. The children might find *May, birthday, same, today, rain, made, shape, grape,* and *grain* while reading charts and shared writing. Once the list has been gathered, the words can be sorted into lists based on their spelling. Through this activity children can learn the various ways to spell the long *a* sound.

Phonemic Awareness and Phonics in the Content Areas

In the primary grades, social studies is generally taught by beginning with families, then moving to larger communities. Read-aloud, shared big books, shared and interactive writing, field trips, and class visitors are common ways for young children to learn about the social studies. Children are invited to respond to social studies experiences through conversations, art, mapmaking, and writing. We do not recommend interrupting social studies lessons to teach phonemic awareness or phonics, but it is appropriate to remind children of their knowledge and to use this knowledge to read and write.

Social studies reading materials add to the child's store of known books. Rereading of these texts should be encouraged as appropriate during the literacy block. The social studies reading materials can then be a resource for teaching phonics and phonemic awareness. By using these materials, teachers are clearly demonstrating authentic purposes for this knowledge.

Many science lessons in the early primary grades involve hands-on experiences and observation. As children explore and make observations, conversations naturally occur. These conversations often lead to writing and drawing. Young children learn to label the parts of plants, insects, and so on. They also learn to tell the personal stories of classroom pets and experiences.

Watching caterpillars change into butterflies is a common practice in primary science. One first-grade class had been carefully observing a caterpillar eat milkweed leaves. In his science journal, Alex wrote the following observations:

he poops a lot
he is a pattern

Alex then carefully drew a picture to illustrate his writing. No book read by the class had mentioned either fact, so the class set about collecting its own data. The children used the data to write a book. References to their own book brought fast, intimate recall of how text was constructed. The very personal nature of this kind of writing makes it appealing to children, and thus, inviting material to use as a basis for learning about phonemic awareness and phonics. By using the book as a teaching tool, the teacher was able to reinforce phonics use and to show children the value of phonics knowledge.

In his observation, Alex made a connection between science and math. Patterns had been the subject of math lessons for several days before Alex's observation. Making connections is something Alex had come to understand. Alex was able to use his knowledge of how words work to correctly spell the message he wanted to write. Teaching skills in isolation deprives children of the broader, deeper understandings to be gained when learning is connected.

Children who have not come to these understandings on their own can be led to these understanding by the teacher. Through explicit teaching and thoughtful questions and conversations, children can learn the value of thinking across and through various concepts. Phonemic awareness and phonics concepts are valuable only as they are used to support reading and writing authentic texts. By helping children connect them to reading and writing, teachers are encouraging children to maximize their use.

Classrooms That Foster Phonics Instruction

In this chapter we have talked about classrooms that use quality children's books and children's writing to foster phonics instruction. In the following chapters we will ask you to "visit" classrooms from pre-kindergarten through second grade. These classroom snapshots will describe children and teachers gaining phonemic awareness and phonics in authentic context.

As you read these chapters, we ask that you consider what each classroom must look like. The classrooms we describe are places where children have built the print-rich environment. Think about the support these print-rich classrooms offer children as they learn about phonemic awareness and phonics.

Chapter 7

Instruction at the Prephonemic Stage

The goal is to help children move from where they are to somewhere else by empowering them to do what they can do and helping them engage in activities through which they can learn more.

(Clay 1998, p. 87)

Phonemic awareness begins to emerge in children as young as three and four years old. Knowing this, preschool teachers can follow the lead of the children to support them in this learning. The fear of "pushing down the curriculum" prevents some preschool teachers from fostering the growth of phonemic awareness in the children they serve. A tour of Ms. Douglas's preschool classroom might assuage these fears.

A Classroom Schedule

One Tuesday morning, a visitor in Ms. Douglas's preschool class found three- and four-year-old children engaged in various activities. Three children were building a farm with wooden blocks. Their conversation was lively and involved.

The children in the kitchen area had decided to play restaurant. There were two customers, a waitress, and a cook. Each child had taken on a role: The cook consulted a cookbook, the waitress made rows of scribbles on her paper, and as the waitress took their order, the customers chatted happily.

In another area of the room, two boys used puppets to act out the story of the *Three Billy Goats Gruff*. The boys used a small table to serve as the bridge. They changed voices for the various characters and took great delight in defeating the mean troll.

Four children were seated at a table with the teaching assistant. They were drawing and discussing pictures, then writing about their drawings. Two of these children were able to write their names. Two wrote streams of letterlike shapes across the bottom of the page.

These children described were engaged in free play. A visitor to Ms. Douglas's classroom who had arrived at the beginning of the day would have found the entire class sitting in a circle singing a good-morning greeting. The children sometimes worked and played as a whole group. At other times, they were assigned to small temporary groups, or were asked to self-select a group to join. There were also opportunities to work and play individually. The teacher and assistant interacted with the children continually.

The four-hour preschool day was active and engaging. Ms. Douglas planned the day to accommodate many learning experiences. Approximately one hour was spent in free play (one-half hour as the children arrived and one-half hour at the end of the day). Whole-group activities filled approximately another hour and a half, with centers and small-group work for an additional hour. Recess and snack filled the remaining half hour.

Ms. Douglas's schedule changes throughout the year but usually looks something like this:

8:00–8:30	Arrival and free play (self-selected group)
8:30–8:45	Good morning song and read-aloud (whole group)
8:45–9:00	Science/social studies concepts (whole group)
9:00–10:00	Center time (small group)
10:00–10:30	Recess and snack
10:30–10:45	Shared reading (whole group)
10:45–11:15	Math concepts (whole group)
11:15–11:45	Free play (self-selected group)
11:45–12:00	Circle time (whole group)

As the children joined Ms. Douglas and the teaching assistant on the rug at 8:30, Ms. Douglas began singing the good morning song. This song served to focus attention and to signal the beginning of the more formal part of the day. The song was used to help the children become acquainted with each other. Ms. Douglas began by singing, "Good morning to you. Good morning to you. Good morning Janelle. Good morning to you." Janelle responded by repeating the song and directing her good morning to another child in the class. All children joined in the singing with Janelle to the classmate she chose to greet. The song was repeated until each child had been greeted. Once the children knew each other well, Ms. Douglas started the day with other songs. Appendix H, Resources for Teachers, includes sources of songs.

Instructional Contexts for Phonemic Awareness

Listening in on Ms. Douglas during read-aloud, we heard her read *Peanut Butter and Jelly: A Play Rhyme* (Westcott 1987). Ms. Douglas read the text while the assistant led the children in the "Peanut butter, peanut butter, Jelly, jelly" refrain. In future readings of the book, Ms. Douglas would teach the children hand motions to accompany the text. After reading the story, Ms. Douglas opened a small box that had been sitting by her chair. She told the children there were some items in the box that had the same beginning sound as *jelly,* and some with the same beginning sound as *peanut.* As she pulled each item from the box (a pencil, a plastic pig, a jump rope, a jelly bean), the children determined if the item sounded like *peanut* or *jelly.*

For the past three days Ms. Douglas had been reading the big book *Mrs. Wishy Washy* (Cowley 1990) during shared reading time. During the first reading of the story, the children chimed in "Wishy, Washy. Wishy, Washy." They took great delight in the illustration of the pig being washed. After the first reading, the children requested that she read the story again. As she read the book a second time, the children joined in on more of the story. Soon most children could read along as Ms. Douglas reread *Mrs. Wishy Washy.* Appendix H lists sources of current books.

Ms. Douglas set up an activity center where children could reenact the story. She placed a bucket of mud alongside a bucket of water and provided plastic animals. The children donned aprons, just like Mrs. Wishy Washy has, and retold the story as the animals were placed in the "lovely mud," and then "wishy washed."

At another activity center the children chose paper animals and finger painted them with lovely mud. They then used their animals at the puppet theater as they reenacted the story. Ms. Douglas served as an audience for the children. She took careful notes about the storytellers.

Each day Ms. Douglas or the teaching assistant sat at the writing center. Conversation was encouraged as children learned to compose stories. The stories were often represented by drawings. At times the children attempted to write down a message, at other times they dictated their stories to the teacher. Other activity centers focused on math, science, and art.

A variety of activities were included during the time set aside each day for teaching phonemic awareness. Many of the shared reading books contained rhyming words. On the day of our visit, Ms. Douglas carefully explained that rhyming words are words that sound almost the same. She gave several examples, with a few children adding their own. After rereading the story together, Ms. Douglas asked the children to listen for the rhyming words. They went through a book listening for words that sound almost the same.

During the discussion of rhyming words, some of children made the connection to nursery rhymes they had memorized. Later Ms. Douglas wrote the nursery rhymes the children had suggested to her on large chart paper. The children illustrated them, and she included them in the shared reading library.

Joey and Janelle discovered that Jack in the nursery rhyme

Jack be nimble,
Jack be quick,
Jack jumped over
The candlestick.

had the same sound in the beginning as their names. Other children soon showed interest in finding other words with the same initial consonant sound as their names. The children also used these familiar rhymes to listen for rhyming words.

Ms. Douglas often played sound games with the children. She asked the children to line up for recess by saying, "If your name begins like *milk* you may line up. Who's in line?" Mark and Makala said their names. The children repeated, "milk, Mark, Makala" to listen for the same first sound. Appendix H has additional sound games resources.

The children also sang along with recordings. Ms. Douglas and the children find music an enjoyable way to learn. See Appendix H for recommended sources of music.

Instructional Contexts for Letter Awareness

Ms. Douglas knows that games are valuable learning experiences, but she also knew she needed to help the children make the bridge from the games to text. When the children were reading the old jump roping rhyme *Miss Mary Mack* during shared reading, Ms. Douglas reminded them of the activity as they lined up. The children related the sound at the beginning of *milk, Mark* and *Makala* to the sound at the beginning of *Miss Mary Mack* and the printed letter *M*.

Ms. Douglas capitalized on the egocentric nature of children and used their names as a starting place for phonemic awareness instruction. Their name chart, shown in Figure 7.1, was a valuable teaching tool.

Figure 7.1 Name Chart

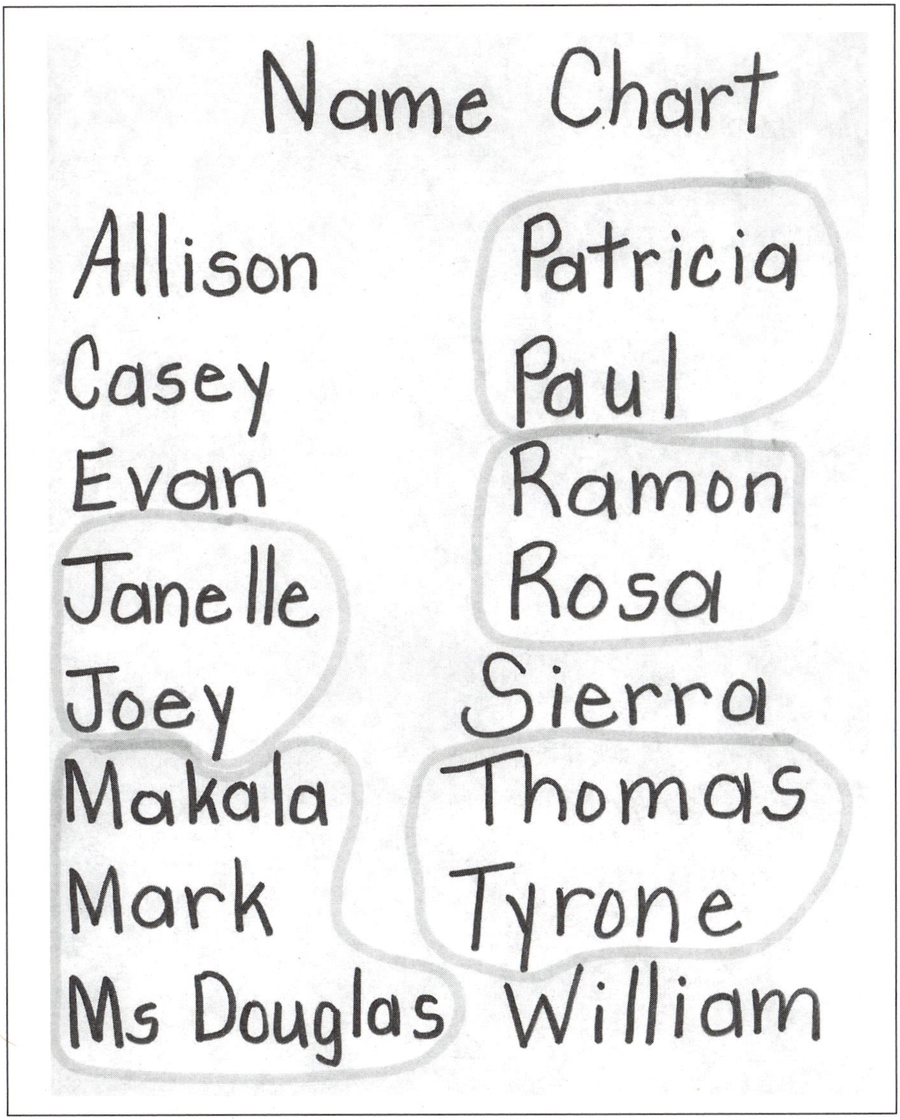

Name Chart

Allison   Patricia
Casey   Paul
Evan   Ramon
Janelle   Rosa
Joey   Sierra
Makala   Thomas
Mark   Tyrone
Ms Douglas   William

There were many opportunities to learn about phonics and phonemic awareness during shared reading of interactive writings and shared writings the children composed. Capitalizing on the familiarity of their own names and compositions, Ms. Douglas helped some children make the letter/sound connection.

Accommodating Individual Differences

Ms. Douglas was a careful observer of the children in her charge. She kept observational records and collected samples of the children's drawings and writing (see Figure 7.2). The notes and samples for each child

Figure 7.2 Drawing and Writing Samples

were stored in a file folder. Ms. Douglas dated the work and notes. As she reviewed the materials in each folder, Ms. Douglas looked for evidence of growth, and took note of what each child needed next. From these work samples Ms. Douglas noticed that Mark, Joey, and Allison had demonstrated an awareness of print and how it works. She decided to conduct more formal assessments for these three children, as shown in Figure 7.3. As observations indicate other children have made similar strides, Ms. Douglas will assess these children also. At mid-year, all children will be assessed.

During center time on this Tuesday, Ms. Douglas sat on the floor with Joey, Allison, and Mark. The class had planned a field trip for the following morning. They planned to visit a working farm, complete with sheep and an apple orchard. During morning share time Ms. Douglas told the children details of the trip. As the children were leaving the sharing circle, Joey remarked that they needed to make a list of all the things to do before they left. Making lists is how Joey's mother organizes her time and materials. Ms. Douglas saw Joey's request for a list as an opportunity. She knew there would be other children interested in the activity. She knew Joey, Allison, and Mark could recite all the letters of the alphabet. They could write their names with ease, and were good at rhyming games. They were often in the library corner where they pretend-read shared reading and other books.

Ms. Douglas's careful observations and assessments led her to feel these children were ready to take on the task of list making. She knew

Figure 7.3 Knowledge of Letters and Letter Sounds

Taken from the Class Record

Date: Oct. 5

Name	No. of Letters Known	Letters Unknown/ Confused	No. of Sounds Known	Sounds Unknown/ Confused
Allison	Upper <u>19</u>/26 Lower <u>18</u>/26	G, H, J, K, P, Q, R; g, j, k, p, q unknown b/d, i/l confusion	Upper <u>17</u>/26 Lower <u>16</u>/26	E, G, J, O, I, Q, U, X, Y; e, g, j, o, i, u, x, y, h unknown
Joey	Upper <u>22</u>/26 Lower <u>18</u>/26	G, Q unknown M/W, b/d, i/l, p/q confusion	Upper <u>18</u>/26 Lower <u>17</u>/26	C, E, Q, Y, X, O, G, Z; e, q, y, x, o, g, z unknown b/d confusion
Mark	Upper <u>21</u>/26 Lower <u>21</u>/26	G, I, J, K, Q; g, i, j, k, q unknown	Upper <u>15</u>/26 Lower <u>15</u>/26	G, J, E, I, U, Q, X, C, K, V, Z; g, j, e, i, q, x, k, v, z unknown b/d confusion

she would need to do most of the scribing but that these children knew some letters and could contribute to the list. As they sat together, the children decided the first item on the list was to be *1. Don't forget your jacket.* Ms. Douglas and the children began by repeating the sentence slowly. Then Ms. Douglas said, "If I want to write this sentence, the first word I need to write is *don't.*" She then proceeded to write on large chart paper *don't* while saying the word slowly. "What will come next?" she asked the children. "Forget," they said in unison. "I know *F,*" said Allison in an excited voice, "My brother's name is Frank, and so is my Dad's." As Allison came to the chart to write the *f,* Ms. Douglas reminded the children that they needed to leave a space between their words so that readers would know where one word ended and the other began. As the writing proceeded, Joey wrote the *j* in *jacket* and Mark added the period at the end of the sentence. They reread the sentences many times. The teacher and children continued to write and talk as they completed the second reminder, *2. Bring your lunch.* As they began the third sentence, *3. Wear comfortable shoes,* Ms. Douglas reminded the children once again of the need to leave a space between words. Joey asked what happened if you forgot to leave the space. After Ms. Douglas's explanation, Joey laughed and said, "Let's write it all together so they will have to read it like this 'wearcomfortableshoes.'" Joey and his friends saw this as amusing; Ms. Douglas saw it as another opportunity. Ms. Douglas wrote the sentence as Joey had suggested. She then cut the words apart so they could be separated and then put back together as the children reread their story. Ms. Douglas asked the three children to illustrate each sentence on the list.

Before the end of the day, the children came together on the rug for circle time. Joey, Mark, and Allison read their list to the class. Joey gleefully demonstrated how to read the last sentence with the words together, and with spaces between them. The class laughed along with Joey.

The next morning, Ms. Douglas asked the class to read the list with her in a shared reading lesson. The children read:

1.   Don't forget your jacket.

"That's my *J,*" said Joey proudly. "That's right," said Ms. Douglas, "Let's say *jacket* and *Joey.* They sound the same in the beginning. Ms. Douglas wrote the letter *J* on a white board. "This is the letter *J,*" she said, "Let's say it again, *jacket, Joey.*" She held the white board directly under the *j* in *jacket.* "Does anyone else have the *j* sound in their name?" she asked. "I do," said Janelle. Ms. Douglas had the children say *Janelle, Joey,* and *jacket* and listen for the first sound. Her instructional focus was to foster the children's ability to discriminate sounds. For the children who were ready to take the step, Ms. Douglas was helping them see the connection between sounds and their visual representations (written letters).

The shared reading lesson continued in this manner with children looking at words and listening for sounds. The list was placed on the wall for the children to look at, read (or pretend to read), and further explore letters and sounds. The illustrations were important cues for some of the children.

Ms. Douglas was pleased by Joey, Mark, and Allison's work. She was also pleased by the interest other children showed in the list. This piece of writing, which could help other children, could now be used for shared reading.

In the week following the field trip, Ms. Douglas's preschoolers had many opportunities to talk about the trip. They drew pictures, dictated stories, and made applesauce. Ms. Douglas noticed several children attempting to write messages about their pictures. She continued to monitor their progress.

As Ms. Douglas reflected, she felt pleased with the literacy learning that had occurred during the farm theme. The children in Ms. Douglas's class had many opportunities to interact with books during shared reading. They were able to participate in the shared reading, and often chose to reread the big books and charts during playtime.

As we end our visit to Ms. Douglas's preschool classroom, consider the tremendous number of literacy experiences the children have had, but also remember the relaxed atmosphere. In this small snapshot of Ms. Douglas's class, we saw many opportunities for children to learn phonemic awareness and phonics, and to see authentic purposes for this learning. Far from forcing a curriculum down, Ms. Douglas has created a classroom where literacy is a natural part of the environment. Literacy tools (cookbooks, telephone directories, notepads, pens/pencils, books, charts, etc.) were available and accessible to the children. Children were engaged in conversations and retellings of stories, often at the theater center and during play. Conversations about books, and the opportunity to explore the language of books, were led by the teacher and the children. Children were encouraged to explore meaning and to expect that books carried meaning.

Ms. Douglas knew the important role of phonemic awareness in learning to read. She used rhyming, songs, and sound games to help the children develop this awareness. She often selected shared reading as a vehicle. The children heard stories and rhymes. Through reading aloud, shared reading, and shared writing, phonemic awareness and phonics activities were always tied to authentic reading experiences. From the beginning, the pre-K children knew there was a *purpose* for learning about phonemic awareness and phonics.

Chapter 8

Instruction at the Emergent Stage

A few items and a powerful strategy might make it easy to learn a great deal more.

(Clay 1991, p. 331)

The children in Ms. Douglas' pre-K class were now ready to join their peers in Ms. Chandler's kindergarten classroom. Ms. Chandler's school administered formal assessments to all entering kindergarten children (see Chapters 3 through 5). Upon completion of the assessment tasks, Ms. Chandler compiled the information in chart form. Like Ms. Douglas, Ms. Chandler used the information gathered from formal assessment and her observations to guide lesson planning.

The formal assessments took place over the first several weeks of the school year. Ms. Chandler used this time to learn more about the children through observation. Once assessments were completed, Ms. Chandler planned the school day.

A Classroom Schedule

A typical kindergarten day was spent in the following activities:

8:00–8:30	Morning circle songs and share time (whole group)
8:30–9:00	Shared or interactive writing (whole group)
9:00–9:30	Read-aloud and shared reading (whole group)
9:30–10:00	Snack and recess
10:00–10:30	Math activities (whole group)

10:30–11:30   Center time
               (small group)
11:30–12:00   Circle time
               (whole group)

Appendix I contains an alternative schedule for all-day kindergarten.

Once assessment was completed, Ms. Chandler organized her observations and formal assessment data. She also took another look at her school system's standards. All of this information was used to determine her next teaching steps.

Instructional Contexts for How Words Work

A peek into the classroom one Thursday in September found Ms. Chandler and the children building a name chart together. They rebuilt the chart for several days. With the children sitting in a group on the rug, Ms. Chandler gave each child a card with his or her name neatly printed on it. She then wrote the letter *A* on a small white board and held it up for the children to see. She used this opportunity to illustrate with words and in writing the correct formation of the letters. She asked anyone with the letter *A* at the beginning of their names to stand at the front of the group. The children looked at Ms. Chandler's *A,* then at the first letter in the name of each child at the front to check for *A.* Once the children had confirmed the *A,* Ms. Chandler taped the names (in alphabetical order) on a large sheet of chart paper. The following day, Ms. Chandler had removed the names from the chart and repeated the procedure. Once the children were able to complete this task with ease, Ms. Chandler once again removed the names from the chart. This time, she asked the children to come to the front of the group if their name had the same *sound* as in the beginning of *apple.* Antonio and Alex came to the front and their name cards were taped to the chart. Ms. Chandler continued in this way until all names were on the chart. This procedure was repeated over several days. A picture of each child was placed beside his or her name. The picture gave the children visual cues to assist in the reading of names.

Ms. Chandler made name puzzles for the children by writing each child's name on strips of tag board and then cutting the letters apart. She taught the children to reassemble the letters from left to right. The children learned that the letters must be in a special order to spell their names. They practiced assembling their name puzzles in the correct order while saying each letter aloud.

From these beginnings, Ms. Chandler continued to help the children see patterns in words. While she understood the usefulness of teaching about word "families," Ms. Chandler understood the danger of overemphasizing structured word patterns. She wanted the children to understand that words work in a variety of ways, and that they needed to be flexible in the use of word knowledge.

The decision was made that kindergarten children in the school needed to learn ten high-frequency words during the school year. Each kindergarten teacher needed to teach and assess the learning of these words. Ms. Chandler chose to support this learning through reading and writing activities. She asked the children to find and frame the words, to practice building and writing the words at center time, and to find the words in previous writing pieces. Since many of the words, such as *the,* did not follow a structured pattern, children would need to learn them by sight. Because they appeared with great regularity in reading and writing, the children needed to read and write the words fluently.

The was the word being practiced on the day of our visit. Ms. Chandler had pointed out the word during shared reading time. Several children had been given the opportunity to frame the word. The class looked at each letter and spelled it aloud. During center time, the children matched magnetic letters to a model, then wrote *the* on dry erase boards. During writing center time, Ms. Chandler asked the children to read their writing. After everyone had finished, the small group then looked to see who had used *the* in their stories. Examples were shared at circle time at the end of the day. Ms. Chandler did not insist that everyone use *the* in their writing for the day. She wanted the children to focus on what they wanted to say, and trust that she would offer them the tools to express themselves.

Instructional Context for Teaching Phonics in Reading

Ms. Chandler knew she needed to help the children build a large repertoire of known reading materials. She read aloud to the children each day, often rereading favorites. Attention was drawn to the sounds of words and phrases. The special language of books was a constant topic of conversation.

The children reread *Mrs. Wishy Washy* (Cowley 1990) and many of the poems and nursery rhymes they had learned at home and in pre-K. Children who knew these texts were instrumental in assisting other children as they became familiar with words and texts. They began to notice the sounds and letters in these familiar shared reading experiences.

Before the school year began, Ms. Chandler had spent some time reading poetry books for children. She selected several poems she thought children would enjoy hearing and reading. She selected the poems based on their quality because Ms. Chandler knew that quality reading material would contain all the examples she would need to help the children learn phonemic awareness and phonics. As the children became familiar with texts, new texts were introduced. Ms. Chandler knew that these materials would serve as the base for explicit teaching.

During shared reading experiences, Ms. Chandler laid the foundation for future reading instruction. She allowed the children large amounts of time to discuss the pictures in the texts. She wanted the children to understand that reading is about getting meaning. These young readers would need to learn to search the pictures for clues to the meaning of the stories. Ms. Chandler also knew that even children who could recite letters didn't necessarily connect this knowledge to the reading of text. Once meaning was in place, she knew she could take some time to help children make this important connection.

Ms. Chandler used the shared reading materials to show children how printed text works. She also used the materials to listen for initial and final consonant sounds, often connecting the new learning to the children's names.

One Thursday morning, while rereading their favorites, the children were asked to listen for words that had the same beginning sound as *Kim.* The children delighted in finding *king, kids,* and *kind.* Some children noticed that *pink, sink,* and *sleek* had the sound at the end. When asked if they knew other words with this sound, the children went on a search around the room. They added the words *kangaroo, keep, ketchup,* and *kindergarten.* The children also volunteered *karate, cat, candy,* and *car.* Ms. Chandler had anticipated this response and used the opportunity to discuss the two ways to spell the /k/ sound.

Phonics Use in Spelling and Writing

As a knowledgeable teacher, Ms. Chandler knew that emergent readers learn a great deal about reading and how words work through many writing experiences. It seemed to be a time when reading and writing are most closely aligned. The emergent stage is then the ideal time to help children understand the reciprocity between reading and writing.

Shared and interactive writing occurred daily in kindergarten. Ms. Chandler worked with the children to help them compose stories and to recount events. She demonstrated how to get stories recorded on paper. She knew the children needed to learn the many aspects of this complex process, but she knew they could not take it on all at once. During shared and interactive writing, Ms. Chandler selected a focus to emphasize with the children and supplied what they needed to complete the task.

On our Thursday visit, the children were writing down the classroom rules. After a great deal of conversation, the children decided to write "Be kind to everyone." They decided if they were kind to each other, it would not be necessary to write out each unkind act they needed to avoid. Since it was early in the school year, Ms. Chandler decided to focus on hearing and recording the sounds in words. She wrote "1." (for the first rule) without comment. She then asked the children to help her decide how many words she needed to write. After repeating the sentence several times, the children decided there needed to be four words. They told Ms. Chandler the first word was *Be*. The children said the word *be* slowly and listened for the first sound. They told Ms. Chandler *b*. Ms. Chandler wrote the *B* while telling the children she was going to write a capital *B* because it was the first word in the sentence. Since the children were unable to hear any other sounds, Ms. Chandler told them about the *e* as she wrote it.

The lesson continued with the children telling Ms. Chandler what they heard (initial consonants) and Ms. Chandler recording the remaining letters. Because her focus was hearing and recording sounds, Ms. Chandler did not mention spacing or punctuation. These important features would come at another time. As the lesson concluded, Ms. Chandler reminded the children to listen carefully to the sounds in the words they wrote during independent writing. She knew children did not always make these important connections on their own.

During center time Ms. Chandler or her teaching assistant remained at the writing center. They talked with children during the composition and scribing of their writing. The teachers helped the children use and extend their knowledge of words and how they work during this important center time. Children read their writing to the teachers and other children. Figures 8.1 and 8.2 show products of two children's work at the writing center.

Accommodating Individual Differences

From the data, Ms. Chandler determined Chase, Jessica, Eliza, Mary, Josh, and Jonathan were in the prephonemic stage. Children in this stage make random marks while writing, using some letterlike scribbles. She knew these children needed many opportunities to interact with text, and thought they would benefit from opportunities to explore rhymes and play sound games.

As Ms. Chandler worked with the children in a small group, her initial lessons focused on the children's names. She wrote each child's name on a card. The children traced the first letters in their names with

Figure 8.1 Work from the Writing Center

Figure 8.2 Work from the Writing Center

a finger while saying the letter name aloud. Once the children could say and trace the letters in their names, Ms. Chandler gave the children an additional set of letters. She had written the individual letters of the children's names on cards. During the next several lessons, the children learned to match the letter cards to the letters on their name cards. They learned to mix up the letters and put them back in order to spell their names, always saying the letter names as they worked. As the children became fluent with this learning, Ms. Chandler decided it was time to add longer text.

Ms. Chandler used familiar shared reading materials with the group. The familiarity they enjoyed freed them to focus on letters and sounds. For these lessons, Ms. Chandler selected nursery rhymes she had written on large chart paper. Ms. Chandler pointed to each word during the shared reading of *Mary Had a Little Lamb*.

Mary Had A Little Lamb
Mary had a little lamb,
Its fleece was white as snow.
Everywhere that Mary went,
The lamb was sure to go.

She asked Mary to frame a capital *M,* and then to find a lowercase *m* to frame. While Mary framed the letters, the three children said the word *Mary.* They look for other *M*'s on the page, and drew the letter *m* in the air. Along with Ms. Chandler, the children repeated this procedure with several other letters they knew, or partially knew. Ms. Chandler's goal was to help the children become flexible with known letters and to help them become solid in their knowledge of partially known letters. In addition, she knew the children needed to make letter/sound connections. While Ms. Chandler worked with other groups, these children went around the room looking for, and saying aloud, known letters. They also participated in sorting activities, sorting pictures by initial sounds they knew. They matched uppercase and lowercase known letters.

On this same morning, Ms. Chandler met with Roberto, Luke, Nick, Melissa, Megan, and Kim, who were all in the emergent stage of reading. While writing, these children were consistently correct in the use of initial consonants, and often correctly represented final consonants. Using the big book *Our Dad* (Wilhelm 1998) Ms. Chandler covered some words and asked the children to predict what the word would be by looking at the pictures. One page says "Dad likes to play the piano" (see Figure 8.3) and shows a picture of Dad sitting at the piano playing and singing. Ms. Chandler covered the words *play the piano* and asked the children to predict what the words might say. Some children thought the word might

Figure 8.3 Using Pictures to Predict Words

Dad likes to play the piano.

be *sing,* and others thought the words would say *play the piano.* Ms. Chandler asked the children what letter they would expect to see if the word was *sing* and what letter they would expect to see if the word was *play.* The words were uncovered so the children could confirm or revise their predictions. Ms. Chandler repeated this procedure with other big books during shared reading.

These exchanges helped Ms. Chandler accomplish her goal: The children were learning and becoming flexible and fluent with initial consonant sounds. They were learning to predict and confirm. In subsequent lessons, Ms. Chandler covered words in context, leaving only the initial consonant showing. These children were soon able to use their knowledge of initial consonants to help them with both reading and writing. Ms. Chandler was soon able to add lessons that included final consonant sounds.

While Ms. Chandler met with other groups, these children sorted pictures by initial consonant sound and letter. They read familiar shared reading texts to each other. They looked for known letters throughout the texts, repeating the letters and their sounds.

Rosa, Casey, James, Manuel, and Nicole were also in the emergent stage but were less consistent in their ability to accurately represent initial consonants. During their small-group lessons, they practiced picture sorts with Ms. Chandler's help. They listened to shared reading texts and joined in when possible, listening for rhymes and letter sounds.

On this Thursday, Ms. Chandler gave each child his own photograph from the name chart. She asked the children to say their names and listen for the first sound. She placed pictures of a car, a mouse, a jar of jelly, a rope, and a nose on the table. One at a time, she asked the children to name the picture and listen for the first sound. The pictures were then matched with the photograph of the child whose name had the same initial consonant sound. The children then matched their photographs with additional pictures of common objects with the same initial consonant sound.

Alex, Jill, and Antonio entered kindergarten knowing most of the alphabet and many letter sounds. These children were also emergent readers but were in the latter part of the stage. They were consistent in the use of initial and final consonants, made (often inaccurate) attempts to use initial consonant blends, and were regularly adding vowels to words while writing. The vowels were often inaccurate. During their small-group time this Thursday morning, Ms. Chandler decided that blends were the next step for these children. She chose to begin with *bl* to introduce the concept. The color words *blue* and *black* would serve as examples. Ms. Chandler and the children reread the familiar big book, *Brown Bear, Brown Bear* (Martin 1996). Ms. Chandler pointed to the word *blue* and asked the children to read it. She then asked them to read *black*. Ms. Chandler asked the children to say both words aloud. She then asked them what they noticed about the two words. The children replied that both words sounded the same in the beginning. Ms. Chandler had written one word under the other and the children noticed they both began with *bl*. Antonio pointed out that the color chart hanging in the room also had those words. After confirming Antonio's observation, Ms. Chandler pointed out that when these two letters are together, they were called a blend. She explained that both letter sounds are heard when you say the blend.

While Ms. Chandler worked with other groups, this group searched other known texts for *bl* blends. Tomorrow they will share the words they found and the group will examine them.

Ms. Chandler recognized the importance of accurate record keeping. Throughout the lessons just described, she jotted notes as appropriate. She continually observed, made notes, and conducted more formal assessments. Careful record keeping was built into her daily routine. This careful record keeping informed her instruction, and allowed her to maximize her time with each group.

This opportunity to look in on a kindergarten classroom confirms that children are natural learners. They are curious and capable. This classroom was a place where children could feel good about what they know and, with the assistance of a thoughtful teacher, build on that knowledge. The atmosphere supported children as they explored letters and sounds through the use of authentic texts. Shared reading experiences were used often and wisely to assist the children as they learned about letters and sounds in authentic contexts. As a thoughtful teacher, Ms. Chandler was able to support the young children in her charge using many literacy activities.

Chapter 9

Instruction at the Early Stage

My position on good teaching is that it arises out of the understanding teachers have of their craft and never out of prescriptive programs.

(Clay 1998, p. 130)

Like Ms. Chandler, Ms. Lacy was aware that the children entering her first-grade classroom would arrive with a variety of strengths and needs. Some children would enter as readers, some would be well on their way to becoming readers, and others would need a great deal of support in their journey. She was acutely aware of the expectations of school personnel, parents, and the children themselves, who believed that first grade was the time to learn to read.

As a seasoned teacher, Ms. Lacy knew that young children were capable of tremendous growth in one school year. She also knew there was no time to lose. There is much to be taught and learned in first grade. Ms. Lacy was also aware that phonics would play a role in the reading success of her students. With this in mind, she prepared for the school year.

A Classroom Schedule

The principal and teachers at Ms. Lacy's school met and discussed classroom schedules. In order to accommodate all that must fit into a school day, compromise was necessary. The school had committed to preserving two and one-half hours for literacy time each day for each classroom. Ms. Lacy's class schedule for the year demonstrates some compromise.

8:00–8:30	Arrival, morning activities
8:30–9:15	Specials (music, art, PE, media)
9:15–11:30	Literacy

11:30–12:15   Lunch and recess
12:15–1:00   Math
 1:00–2:00   Science and/or social studies

Each morning at 8:00 the children in Ms. Lacy's class took their own attendance by writing their names on a printed sign-in sheet. They then reported their lunch status by clipping clothespins bearing their names to the appropriate spot on a card (see Figure 9.1). Once these morning tasks were completed, the children chose books from the classroom library and read. The children could choose to read along or with others.

By 8:15 all buses had arrived and the children had taken care of their morning status reporting. Two children filled in the report forms for

Figure 9.1 Lunch Status

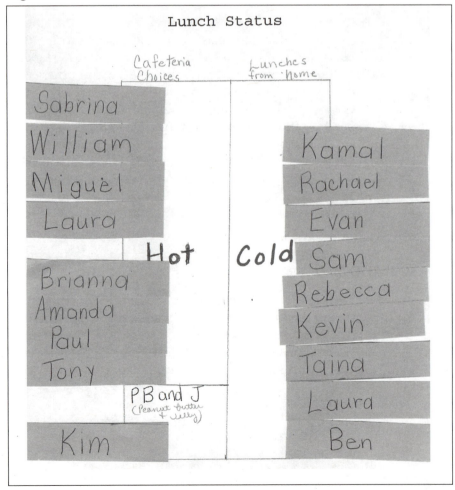

attendance and lunch count and delivered them to the school office. Ms. Lacy and the remaining children met as a group to read and discuss the morning message (see Figure 9.2). Learning opportunities from the morning message set the stage for the day.

Instructional Context for Teaching Phonics in Reading

Many children enter first grade as early readers. Early readers know many letter sounds and some sight words. They are beginning to notice and use letter clusters when encountering unknown words. Picture cues and sentence structure are used as sources of information to maintain meaning.

Early readers begin to develop self-monitoring strategies. They can match text to speech, and can use this knowledge to self-correct (example: Text says "See the dog." Child reads: "See the big dog." Child can self-monitor because she read four words instead of three). Early readers notice when sentences they read don't make sense. They are aware that they need to reread when this occurs, and that they need to find and correct the error. They may also notice mismatches of pictures and text.

Figure 9.2 Morning Message

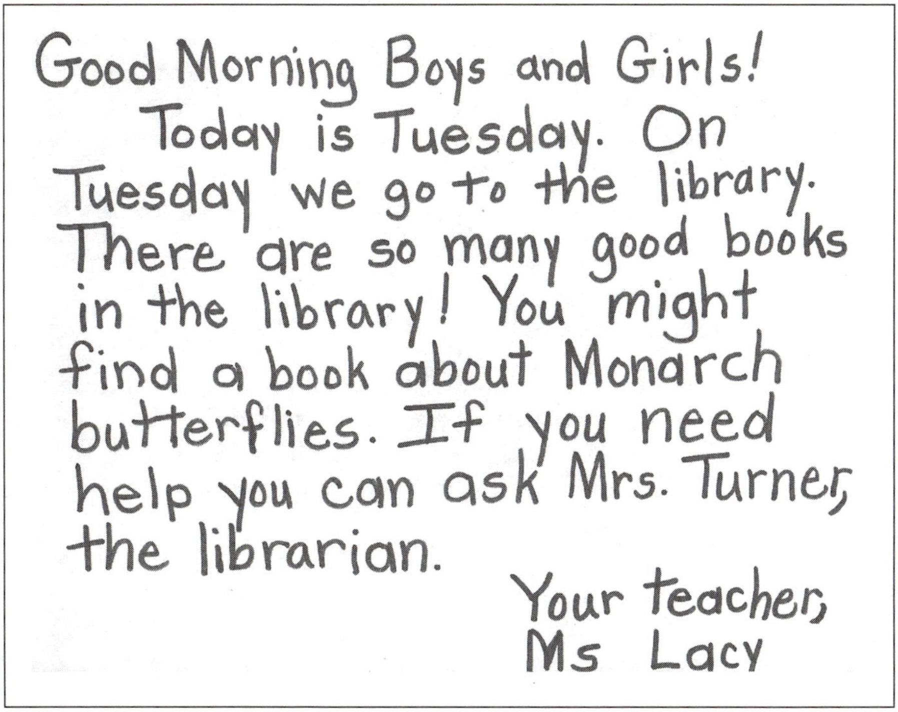

Good Morning Boys and Girls!
    Today is Tuesday. On
Tuesday we go to the library.
There are so many good books
in the library! You might
find a book about Monarch
butterflies. If you need
help you can ask Mrs. Turner,
the librarian.
                Your teacher,
                Ms Lacy

Children who are early readers are using initial and sometimes final consonant sounds to monitor their reading. They also use their knowledge of sight words to help them monitor. These self-monitoring behaviors allow them to maintain meaning and fluency.

As they move through this stage, children become flexible in their use of initial and final consonant sounds. The use of letter clusters and endings is increased. Early readers become more aware of the features of text, and are less dependent on picture cues.

During daily read-aloud time, Ms. Lacy encouraged the children to listen carefully, while encouraging relevant talk throughout the read-aloud time. Children were not asked to sit quietly until the oral reading was complete. Sometimes the children initiated the conversation. In addition, Ms. Lacy often stopped and said to the children, "Let's listen to that part again." As the text was reread, conversation started to flow.

By encouraging talk throughout the reading, Ms. Lacy allowed the children to connect to the text. Some children responded with personal connections, some with connections to other texts, and others could connect the text to other experiences and settings. The children were encouraged to predict, and confirm or revise. They learned to infer from the text and illustrations. The children learned to immerse themselves in text. Ms. Lacy taught the children to respond to text as skillful readers do.

Even during the first few days of school, Ms. Lacy's observations of the children helped her plan appropriate instruction. During shared reading, Ms. Lacy noticed who was able to join in the reading. While constructing a name chart with the children, Ms. Lacy noticed who was aware of the letters and sounds in their own names, and the names of the other children. Ms. Lacy made notes and collected drawings and writing the children completed in the first few days of school.

Phonics Used in Spelling and Writing

While conferring with individual children during writing workshop, Ms. Lacy used the opportunity to support the children as writers. She scaffolded their writing by encouraging them to listen to the sounds in words and record what they heard. She also carefully monitored progress so that as children were led to learn about how words work, they could use this knowledge to move toward conventional spelling.

During shared writing, interactive writing, and writing workshop activities the children were able to compose stories, and use their knowledge of letters and sounds to put their thoughts on paper. Although Ms. Lacy did the actual scribing during shared writing, she talked about her thinking processes while the children watched. A typical conversation might include the fact that Ms. Lacy wanted to write a word she might not know how to spell. She demonstrated how to use what she knew to help her write a word she didn't know.

One Friday morning the beginning of the school day was delayed because of thick smoke coming from a forest fire in the area. It was, of course, a hot topic for conversation and writing. Ms. Lacy helped the children use what they all knew (the sounds of *th*), and what some of the children knew (the letter and sound of short *i*) to write *thick*. Several children noticed that *thick* had the same *ck* at the end as the name of their classmate *Nick*. The children were able to hear and record *smok*. Ms. Lacy added the final *e* and offered a brief explanation of the silent *e* principle.

Ms. Lacy continued to keep careful records of the progress the children made. She looked at writing samples and running records for evidence the children were *using* their phonics skills. She remembered that the purpose of phonics is to help children as they read and write. If no evidence of use was found, she knew she needed to revisit that area of phonics (see Figures 9.3 and 9.4).

Figure 9.3 Evidence of Phonics Use

Figure 9.4 Evidence of Phonics Use

Instructional Contexts for How Words Work

In addition to her observations during shared reading and of writing samples, Ms. Lacy administered some more formal assessments (see Chapters 3 through 5). While assessments were being completed, Ms. Lacy decided to begin phonics instruction. She chose to spend some time at the beginning of the school year reinforcing and, with some children, teaching the initial consonant sounds. She based this decision on her knowledge that children generally learn initial consonant sounds first. During shared reading, she noted that some children were hesitant with their answers. Ms. Lacy's goal was that children be able to use initial consonant sounds fluently and flexibly. Knowing that the children had had many opportunities to learn about initial consonants in nursery school and kindergarten, Ms. Lacy felt she could accomplish this goal quickly, most likely by the time initial assessments were completed.

During shared reading time, Ms. Lacy reread *Mrs. Wishy Washy* (Cowley 1990), "Who has a name with the same beginning sound as Mrs. Wishy Washy?" she asked. "I do!" said William. "I can be William Wishy Washy." Soon all the children were looking for characters in the shared reading texts with the same letter sounds as their names. Kamal and Kevin became *King Kamal* and *King Kevin* after reading *Old King Cole*. Ms. Lacy wrote poems and jump-rope rhymes on large chart paper. During shared reading time the children read the rhymes together, with each child inserting his or her name and other words with the same initial consonant. Ms. Lacy sent home copies for the children to read to their parents.

Ms. Lacy knew it was not necessary or even desirable to use poetry and other books written specifically to teach phonics. The use of high-quality, high-interest reading material motivated the children to want to learn how to read independently. Moreover, authentic reading materials naturally contain all the phonics elements Ms. Lacy and the children needed to learn and practice. They would return to these well-known favorites many times for enjoyment and to practice phonics skills.

Accommodating Individual Differences

Ms. Lacy completed formal assessments as described in Chapters 3 through 5 and compiled the results into a chart. Based on the information gained from this data, Ms. Lacy decided to work with the children in four small groups. These small-group activities were sometimes a part of the guided reading program (Fountas and Pinnell 1996) or were small, temporary groups formed specifically to teach needed phonics skills.

Most of the children in Ms. Lacy's first grade fell into the early reader stage: two children were transitional readers, and three were emergent readers. In order to meet the needs of all children in her classroom, Ms. Lacy divided the early readers into two groups. Some children in this group fell into the first part of the stage and others had moved to the latter part of the stage. Additionally, there would be one group for transitional readers and one for emergent readers.

Tania, Amanda, and Nick entered first grade as emergent readers. During initial observations, Ms. Lacy realized they would need many opportunities to interact with text. While her teaching assistant read aloud to the remainder of the class, Ms. Lacy helped Tania and Nick with many of the activities described in Chapter 8. Ms. Lacy knew that although her teaching assistant was bright and capable, teachers are better equipped to work with the children most in need. It was evident to Ms. Lacy that she would need to accelerate the learning of these children. She knew that these children would need individual instruction when possible.

Alphabet Books

In addition to the activities described in Chapter 8, Ms. Lacy made alphabet books with the three children. They wrote a known letter on each page and selected a picture to represent each letter. Ms. Lacy knew children needed their own pictures to represent each letter. These letter/sound books would be used to help the children make connections to letters in words. These books were useful references for further learning about letters and sounds.

Shared Reading

Shared reading was an integral part of each day's small-group lesson. The children compared the initial sounds in their names and letter/sound pictures to words in the text. Ms. Lacy had the children frame letters (Appendix J contains sample frames) and sort pictures by initial sounds.

While Ms. Lacy continued to work with the children to learn the letters and sounds, she knew they could begin to read and write without knowing *all* the letters and sounds. In addition to their work with phonics, the children read books with repetitive patterns, learned how books work, and built a store of known words. Ms. Lacy used the group time to provide many opportunities for success.

Small-Group Interventions

Ms. Lacy's careful observations and scaffolding enabled the children who had entered first grade at the end of the emergent stage to make steady progress. Since she worked with this group from the beginning of the school year, not waiting for formal assessment to be completed, the children were given opportunities to catch up to their classmates. Ms. Lacy believed in flexible grouping and planned that children in this group would join other groups soon.

A typical lesson with the group began with the children rereading eight to ten familiar texts. Ms. Lacy knew it was vital that these children experience the success and pleasure of rereading. She also knew these books were valuable teaching partners. Since the children were very familiar with the text, their attention would be free to discover new features of the text and illustrations.

Once the rereading was complete, the children's attention was focused on a new text. Ms. Lacy introduced the book and asked the children to join her on a story walk. Ms. Lacy and the children looked at the book cover and each illustration, predicting and inferring about the meaning of the book. When the story walk was completed, children read the text at their own pace. Ms. Lacy listened to each child. She offered support as needed and took careful notes regarding observed reading behaviors and use of phonics.

Brianna, Kevin, Sabrina, Laura, William, and Paul met as a small group for the first time in late September. They had recently entered the early reader stage. Ms. Lacy knew that children at this stage needed to become flexible in the use of known initial and final consonants. They needed to add to this store of known sounds, and learn about blends.

One Wednesday, Ms. Lacy met with the group to read the shared reading text *The Royal Dinner* (Parkes 1988). Since this was a new shared reading text for the group, Ms. Lacy read it to the children. Soon they were able to join in with "or it's OFF WITH YOUR HEAD!" The children asked to read the book again. During the rereading they were able to join in more often. Ms. Lacy then put this book aside. In the future she would use this book to teach phonics lessons, but she knew that the book would need to be less novel before she used it to teach. After reading *The Royal Dinner,* the children reread several favorite shared reading books and poems.

Ms. Lacy selected *Dishy-Washy* (Cowley 1998) for this day's lesson. The book had been a favorite since the children were in kindergarten. Ms. Lacy directed the children's attention to the words *pots and pans* on page 10. They listened for the sound *p* makes at the beginning of those words and in Paul's name. Their attention then turned to page 11 and to the word *plate,* and they discussed blends and the sound of *pl.* Ms. Lacy and the children made a list of other words the children knew with the same initial sound as *plate.* The children added *play, please, plus,* and *plum* to the list. The list was placed on the wall so that words could be added as they were noticed. This activity was followed by picture sorting to contrast the sounds of *p* and *pl.*

During this Wednesday's meeting with Rebecca, Ben, Tony, Kamal, Rachael, and Miguel, Ms. Lacy and the children read the familiar text *Who's in the Shed?* (Parkes 1996). Ms. Lacy had introduced the text at the beginning of the school year so the children were very familiar with the story. They read the story with pleasure.

Based on her knowledge that these children were well into the early reader stage, Ms. Lacy's lesson on this Wednesday was to continue work with medial short vowels. In previous lessons the children had learned about short *a* and short *o*. Short *i* would be today's focus.

Ms. Lacy used magnetic letters to write the word *pig*. She asked the children to read the word. She then removed the *p* and asked the children to read *ig*. Ms. Lacy knew that the use of word families was a proven way to introduce short vowel sounds. Ms. Lacy turned to page 12 in *Who's in the Shed?*, and the children read *"It's something big," grunted the fat pink pig. "It's something big."* The children immediately noticed that *big* and *pig* share the *ig* letters and sound. Ms. Lacy asked the children to find words with *ig* as they reread other familiar shared reading materials. The children identified *dig* and *wig* from the shared reading materials. No one noticed that the first syllable in Miguel's name had the *ig* letters and sounds. Since they didn't notice, Ms. Lacy decided to save the discussion of the connection to syllables for another time. She did, however, note this information for further reflection.

Ms. Lacy wanted the children to be flexible enough to use their new learning in both reading and writing. She knew that children were not always able to make connections on their own. She continued the lesson by talking with the children about a storm on the previous night. They talked about the wind and the rain. Ms. Lacy spoke of the twigs that blew out of the trees and fell in her yard. She told the children she planned to write about the storm during writing time and asked them to help her with the word *twig*. The group said the word slowly, listening for sounds. They knew initial sounds and were able to get *tw* easily. Ms. Lacy pointed out that *twig* had the same middle and ending sounds as *pig*. The group said, *pig, big,* and *twig* together. They decided the last two letters in *twig* were *ig*. Ms. Lacy wrote *twig* on her white board. She then wrote *pig* and *big* in a column under *twig*. The children were able to see how the words were the same (*ig* ending) and how they were different (the beginnings). Ms. Lacy concluded the lesson with the reminder that the children could use known words and word parts to help themselves read and write.

Sam, Kim, and Evan had entered first grade as readers and writers at the transitional stage. They were consistent in their use of consonants and vowels while writing. Ms. Lacy's assessment indicated that Kim and Evan "use but confuse" (Invernizzi, Abouzeid, and Gill 1994) long vowel patterns.

During shared reading with these children, Ms. Lacy asked them to look for words with the letter *e*. During the reading of *Who's in the Shed?*, the children found *shed, led, peep, sheep, hen, then,* and *see*. In other shared readings they found *he, sea, tree, bed, team, leaf, peel, head, me, mean, instead,* and *she*. Ms. Lacy led the children in a word sort.

The children first sorted the words by sound:

Short *e*	Long *e*
shed	peep
led	sheep
hen	see
then	sea
bed	tree
head	team
instead	leaf
	mean
	peel
	she
	me
	he

The group then sorted the words by pattern:

Short *e*		Long *e*		
shed	instead	tree	sea	she
led	head	sheep	leaf	he
hen		peep	mean	me
then		peel	team	
bed		see		

These sorting activities helped the children move beyond simply writing the sound they heard and into thinking about how words work.

Time Management

The first-graders in Ms. Lacy's class spent portions of each day interacting as a group. Sometimes the group included the entire class, but often the children worked in small temporary groups. Time was also set aside each day for independent reading and writing. This varied schedule kept the children both physically and mentally alert. Since she believed children needed these varied opportunities, Ms. Lacy followed a management system that encouraged active learning throughout the day.

Ms. Lacy spent approximately one and one-half hours per day working with small groups of children. As a reflective teacher, she knew the time she spent with the children was both valuable and necessary. Each group spent from twenty to thirty minutes engaged in small-group activities, and the remaining time working independently. The bulk of this time (one hour to one hour and ten minutes) was spent without direct teacher input. Independent authentic learning activities were an important part of the day.

Based on her belief that children need time to practice reading and writing, Ms. Lacy set up the classroom to encourage both. Shelves, baskets, and crates held a wide variety of books with a range of topics and reading difficulty. Children were expected to read several easy books each day. The children could identify these books easily since Ms. Lacy had placed them in color-coded baskets. In addition, they could revisit the class big books, shared reading materials, and read-aloud books. Partner and independent reading occurred during independent work time.

A writing center offered children many opportunities to practice. They often completed journal writings and drew illustrations during this time. Partners were encouraged to read their writing to each other.

At another center, the children practiced appropriate word study activities. Some children were matching uppercase and lowercase letters, others sorted pictures based on initial or final sounds, and others used chunks (*an, ig*) to build and write words. Patterns discussed during group time were practiced at the word study center.

In addition to reading and writing tasks, the children practiced math concepts. Science observations were made and recorded during independent work time. Art and drama centers added to the many possibilities for practice and learning.

Ms. Lacy spent time during the beginning of the school year teaching the children how the centers worked, and how to use the materials. Her goal was that the children be able to complete the activities independently, then move to their next center.

In order to monitor the progress, Ms. Lacy took approximately two minutes between small-group lessons to visit centers. She wanted the children to know she valued the center work and that she was interested in the activities there. In addition, her teaching assistant monitored the centers, often stopping to listen to a child read a story or a piece of writing.

Our view into this busy first-grade classroom showed engaged learners becoming independent readers and writers.

Chapter 10

Instruction at the Transitional Stage

At the transitional level, the reader has developed a range of flexible strategies for working on text. He has acquired an extended reading vocabulary and shows interest in unfamiliar words that are read to him. His decoding skills are more sophisticated and refined; thus he reads longer texts with greater accuracy and fluency.

(Dorn and Soffos 2001, p. 48)

As we enter the second-grade classroom we see Mr. Porter at the overhead projector. He is doing a phonics lesson with a small, guided reading group. Another group of students is gathered around the word wall and pinning up words in a new phonics category they explored in a shared reading lesson. Two students are writing words in columns on chart paper. Other students are working in pairs to edit writing drafts, to write in journals, or to read individually in preparation for a literature study group. This is a typical scene in a classroom with many readers and writers at the transitional phase of literacy development. (See the curriculum in Table 2.1 for key concepts.)

Mr. Porter uses many of the assessments outlined in Chapters 3 and 4 to guide his literacy, including phonics, instruction. He relies particularly on analysis of errors on running records and on writing samples to assess gaps in students' understanding and to plan instruction. We used his class profile to show how one teacher recorded assessment information to give him a class-at-a-glance look at his students (see Table 5.1 in Chapter 5). We will use this class as a reference point throughout this chapter.

Managing the Classroom

Mr. Porter's second grade is typical of many classrooms in which students demonstrate a wide range of literacy development and specific needs. It takes careful planning and well-established routines for a classroom to operate with a variety of individual, small-group, and large-group formats for instruction. However, transitional readers can do so much more reading and writing on their own than students at lower levels. During the reading workshop, second-graders are usually able to work independently on a variety of tasks as the teacher gives attention to individuals or to guided reading or literature study groups. Examples of tasks the second-graders might work on independently include word study activities assigned to them in a previous guided reading lesson, reading independently for a variety of purposes, pursuing a research or inquiry project related to a content area, and writing in journals for a variety of purposes.

Phonics and word study concepts echo across independent study time, guided reading time, writing, and even content area studies. The benefit of an embedded approach is that students apply what they are taught in meaningful reading and writing contexts. In the remaining sections of this chapter we outline how phonics instruction can be embedded in a variety of instructional contexts already occurring in your classroom.

Mr. Porter uses the literacy block of time in the following way:

8:00 Language study
- Read aloud and think aloud
- Genre or author study
- Shared reading
- Vocabulary development and word study

9:00 Reader's workshop
- Guided reading groups
- Literature study groups
- Independent work (e.g., reading in preparation for literature study groups, follow-up work from guided reading group, journal writing for a variety of purposes, research and inquiry projects, familiar rereading practice, word study center, etc.)

10:30 Writer's workshop (about 1 hour)
- Large- and small-group mini-lessons (e.g., conventions, phonics for spelling, genre study, etc.)
- Writing in a variety of genres
- Conferencing (e.g., for topic development, revision, editing)
- Share time

Phonics Instruction in the Context of Language Study

Mr. Porter uses the language study time to do read-alouds, shared reading, and vocabulary development and word study related to the read-aloud or shared reading. The class is currently working on fairy tales as a genre, and he read them *The True Story of the Three Little Pigs* (Scieszka 1989). It's a hilarious revision of the story from the wolf's point of view. After reading the story aloud, Mr. Porter and the class discussed how other familiar fairy tales could be rewritten from a different character's point of view. He encouraged them to try doing this for their fairy tales.

Then, Mr. Porter continued with a whole-group vocabulary and word study lesson on possessives—nouns and pronouns that show ownership. Mr. Porter noticed in an analysis of students' writing samples that most did not know how to use apostrophes in possessives. Possessives are typically studied by transitional readers in the syllable-juncture stage, but Mr. Porter reasoned that because students were using plurals already, it would make sense to them. In addition, he knew he could use an editing conference to reinforce the concept with anyone who continued to have difficulty with possessives. Here's how the lesson went:

Mr. Porter found several sentences in the book that contained the apostrophe *s* denoting ownership: *granny's birthday cake, neighbor's house, Little Pig's brother, wolf's honor.* He copied these sentences onto an overhead transparency and said, "I noticed that many of you are not sure how to show that someone owns something—like Jennifer's barrette or Jason's cars—in your writing. I'm going to show you how authors do this by showing you some sentences from the book I just read to you." Then, he showed the sentences, one by one and helped the students notice how the apostrophe was used. He also wanted the students to understand the difference between this use of the apostrophe *s* as a possessive and instances where *s* is used as a plural and as a contraction (*that's, it's*) so he went back to *The True Story of the Three Little Pigs* to find examples of these usages and again copied them onto an overhead and showed them to the students.

Mr. Porter made a mental note to follow up on the lesson in guided reading groups by having students locate possessives. He also made a note in his records that he had taught possessives in a whole-group lesson.

Instructional Contexts for Phonics in Reader's Workshop

There are various ways you might approach phonics instruction during reader's workshop. First, you might teach small groups of students who appear to need help using specific phonics patterns. For example, Mr. Porter discovered through running record analyses and the Names Test that Jeremy, Michael, Sarah, Maria, Jerome, and Melanie all needed help with *ew,* even though they were not reading at the same instructional levels or in the same guided reading groups. He called these students together during the reader's workshop to do a quick phonics lesson using shared reading.

Shared Reading

There are many texts you could use to make explicit how /ew/ works as a sound pattern in words. Mr. Porter chose to use three short poems from the book, *Talking Like the Rain: A Read-to-Me Book of Poems* (Kennedy and Kennedy 1992), which the class had heard as a read-aloud. The words *blew, flew,* and *dew* were used in the poems. He made overhead transparencies of the three poems. To teach the lesson, Mr. Porter did the following:

- Mr. Porter read the poems with the students, as in any shared reading.
- Mr. Porter highlighted the targeted words with the /ew/ sound in each poem with an overhead pen.
- The students generated other words with the /ew/ sound, which they wrote (with a minimum of help) on a blank overhead transparency: *crew, stewardess, review, brew,* and *grew,* among others.
- Mr. Porter used words generated by the students to review or extend known concepts. For example, the word *stewardess* gave him an opportunity to review how known spelling patterns can be used to analyze longer words by analogy (i.e., *stew* as in *few, ar* as in *car, dess* as in *mess*). For another example, the students suggested ways to turn the other words into longer words, such as *brew* into *brewer.* Again, it gave Mr. Porter a chance to review word-building principles taught in an earlier lesson.
- As independent work, Mr. Porter asked students to write all the /ew/ words in the poems and the ones they had generated, both the base words and the words with additions, on tag board strips. The strips were posted on the word wall under a new /ew/ column. Jerome volunteered to tell the whole class about the addition of the column during the final class meeting of the day.

The lesson itself took about fifteen minutes; the writing of words on strips and posting on the wall were done independently by the students while Mr. Porter moved on to another small group. He pulled together Adrian, Jessica, Darnel, Sierra, and Josh for a similar shared reading lesson on /aw/ and /au/ using other short poems from the same familiar read-aloud book. Mr. Porter made a note in the instructional records he kept on each student to indicate he had covered these phonics patterns.

Guided Reading

Jenna and Darrell are reading at text level O (32/34). They form a small guided reading group. Their assessments indicated they were very proficient with many phonics concepts in both reading and writing. Their knowledge of patterns in single-syllable words was secure, enabling them to read and write these words automatically. Although they had been reading and writing polysyllabic words for some time, Mr. Porter's assessments suggested they were at the syllable-juncture stage. He wanted to be sure he had made explicit the concept of doubling the consonant in short vowel, single-syllable words when adding endings beginning with a vowel (e.g., *ed, ing, en, er*).

Mr. Porter chose the book *My Rotten Redheaded Older Brother* (Polacco 1994) for a guided reading lesson that spanned across two days. The book had been a favorite read-aloud with the whole class; Mr. Porter judged that Jenna and Darrell would be capable of reading the book themselves, especially given that they had heard the story once. The book tells of sibling rivalry and one-upmanship from a young girl's point of view. The main characters include the young girl, her "rotten redheaded older brother" who can do everything better, and Bubbie, the mediating grandmother.

Mr. Porter met with Jenna and Darrell as soon as reader's workshop began on the first day of the two-lesson sequence. He reviewed with them the story line and sent them off to eagerly read the book to themselves. After meeting with two other guided reading groups, Mr. Porter again called Jenna and Darrell up to meet with him. They enthusiastically shared their favorite parts of the book. Then, Mr. Porter used the book as an opportunity for literature study to extend Jenna's and Darrell's understanding of characterization.

On the following day, Mr. Porter used the book for a second guided reading lesson on phonics. Through an informal spelling assessment and analysis of errors they made on running records and writing samples, Mr. Porter evaluated Jenna and Darrell to be at the syllable-juncture stage. Using the curriculum as a guide, he is systematically teaching them concepts from that phase in the context of their guided reading lessons. Even though Jenna and Darrell read many polysyllabic words in the context of continuous text with ease, he wants to bring syllable-juncture concepts to their attention. The concept he is teaching them in today's lesson is doubling the consonant before adding endings. Mr. Porter made overhead transparencies of a couple of pages from the book that had examples of words illustrating the principle of doubling the consonant before adding endings (e.g., *slapped, setting, rotten*). The pages also had examples of words in which the consonant was not doubled (e.g., *starting, watched, pulling, older, teased*). We do not include the text here because the format for instruction would be the same regardless of the choice of materials. The lesson went something like this:

- Mr. Porter, Jenna, and Darrell each read two pages from the text shown on the overhead transparencies, taking turns at being the characters in the story. Mr. Porter does not always begin the lesson this way, but this story was written with clear sections where the grandmother, the older brother, or the young girl is speaking.
- The pages were read again to emphasize expression and fluency and just for fun.
- Mr. Porter began his lesson with an explanation about doubling the consonant on a short-vowel word before adding an ending beginning with a vowel. He used the term *CVC pattern* because Jenna and Darrell are used to describing orthographic patterns using C to indicate consonants and V to indicate vowels in a spelling pattern.
- He located and framed the CVC base word in each of the target words—*slap* in *slapped, set* in *setting,* and *rot* in *rotten*—writing "CVC" over each base word. Then, he slid the frame open to show the extra consonant before the ending. Mr. Porter made the frame by gluing together two rectangular pieces of tag board to cover a portion of text. He cut out a "window" just long enough and high enough to reveal two to three words at a time. He slid a thin strip of tag board between the two pieces of tag board so that it could cover the "window" or be moved to reveal words or pieces of words. It allows the teacher and students to "zoom in" on details in the print. Appendix J contains directions for making a sliding mask.
- Mr. Porter used a blank overhead and demonstrated how to add endings on other simple, one-syllable words with the CVC pattern (e.g., *sit/sitting, dip/dipped, pat/patting*).
- Mr. Porter asked Jenna and Darrell to suggest other one-syllable words with the CVC pattern, letting them write the words on the overhead transparency and practice adding endings.
- Coincidentally, both Jenna and Darrell's names have double consonants before vowels, which they were quick to point out. Mr. Porter explained that Jenna's name followed the double-the-consonant principle: *Jen* into *Jenna.* Then he explained that Darrell's name was an exception, as names often are. That is, *Darrell* is spelled differently from other names that sound like it (e.g., *Carol* and *Harold*)

and does not follow the typical pattern for adding endings to words that sound like or are spelled like the first syllable in *Darrell* (e.g., *care/cared* and *bare/bared*). Although, *Darrell* is spelled like the words *barrel* or *barren*. Mr. Porter gave a cursory explanation of *r*-controlled vowel patterns and made a mental note to use Darrell's name as an example in a later lesson on *r*-controlled spelling patterns. He also resolved to bone up on principles taught at the derivational-constancy stage. This is the last stage of spelling development and is more typical for upper elementary and middle schoolers. In this stage orthographic considerations (sound-spelling connections) give way to morphological considerations (meaning-spelling connections). Morphology is helpful in explaining why many words that appear to have a similar orthography for the base word may be spelled differently because of different meanings.

- Mr. Porter returned to the shared reading text and located words with other consonant-vowel patterns and also had endings (e.g., *meeting*—CVVC, *pulling*—CVCC, *older*—VCC). He used the frame again to display the consonant-vowel pattern in the base word, and wrote the pattern over the word using an overhead projector marker.
- Finally, Mr. Porter asked Jenna and Darrell to make columns on a piece of flip-chart paper for each consonant-vowel pattern discussed in today's lesson. He instructed them to write under the appropriate category the target words and examples generated in the lesson.

This lesson took about twenty minutes. Jenna and Darrell completed the word-sort chart independently. Mr. Porter planned to use the chart to review the concept in editing conferences during writing workshop or in guided reading lessons. He also planned to add another category to the chart, CVCe, when he taught the concept of dropping *e* from words before adding endings (e.g., *tape/taping*). Jenna and Darrell also continued to add words to the categories as they encountered them in reading and writing. Mr. Porter made a note in his guided reading group records that he had taught this concept to Jenna and Darrell.

Another Guided Reading Group

Mr. Porter met with Alex, Danielle, Spencer, Miranda, and Nathan as a group for guided reading at the G (11/12)/H (13/14) levels. They were all having difficulty decoding written words in a systematic way, and the Names Test indicated they were unfamiliar with many sound/symbol patterns. Confirming this, their spelling and writing assessments indicated they were still using letter sounds, rather than orthographic patterns, as their primary strategy for spelling. Their assessments indicated they were typical of students at the beginning of the transitional/within-word-pattern phase of reading development, but they had many gaps in using concepts from the early/within-word-pattern phase of phonics development.

Mr. Porter chose a challenging text at Level H (14), *Goodnight Moon* (Brown 1975), to use for the lesson. The book would be challenging for this group, because it had many words they would have to figure out. However, the pictures gave many clues, and Mr. Porter gave an exceptionally thorough introduction to the book. Before they read the book to themselves, the students were very familiar with the ideas, the rhyming language pattern, and some words he thought might be unknown concepts, such as *mush*. Mr. Porter chose this book because of the many rhyming patterns; the concept he wanted to teach the students was that words that look alike at the end often sound the same, and if you know a pattern in one word, that will help you figure out other words. This is probably the most important concept students learn in the within-word-pattern phase.

Mr. Porter watched as the students read so he could intervene and teach when they encountered difficulties. Danielle had difficulty with *mush* and *hush,* words that she couldn't get through meaning. Mr. Porter used a small white board to show her the *ush* phonogram and then helped her figure out *brush.* Nathan had trouble with *comb,* but he figured it out from the picture. Mr. Porter quickly showed him how *b* on the ends of some words, like *lamb,* are silent.

When the children finished reading silently, they discussed their interpretations. Then, Mr. Porter and the students did a choral reading of the book so they could hear the rhymes and feel the rhythm of the language. Finally, Mr. Porter moved into his phonics concept lesson. He asked the students to locate all the pairs of rhyming words throughout the book, and he wrote them on chart paper. They discussed the patterns they saw emerging. For each group of rhyming words with a common phonogram, Mr. Porter added a word and helped the students use the two known words to figure out the new word. He let the students dictate more new words in each group that sounded like the known words on the chart, and Mr. Porter wrote them so the group could see if the pattern followed. In some cases, it didn't (e.g., *bear* and *chair*), and this led to a discussion of irregular patterns.

As a follow-up activity, Mr. Porter directed the children to copy the groups of rhyming words into a new section in their word journals, and he challenged them to add one word to each group. He planned to come back to the journals at the end of the day, after the children left, to see if they had learned the principle of applying patterns. He planned to begin the next day's guided reading group by asking students to read some groups of words from their journals. And, he would remind them to use what they knew about patterns to help them figure out new words as they read their new books.

Phonics Instruction in the Context of Writer's Workshop

Mini-lessons and writing conferences provide the vehicles for phonics instruction in writer's workshop. Again, using the curriculum as a guide, Mr. Porter uses whole-group phonics mini-lessons to teach the class about phonics concepts for spelling. This ensures that he stays slightly ahead of students' current understandings in order to lead their development forward. In Mr. Porter's school, the primary teachers have adopted the developmental phonics curriculum; each teacher systematically teaches phonics for spelling, as outlined for their grade levels.

The phonics curriculum is the foundation of this school's spelling program, supplemented by lists of high-frequency words (i.e., words used most frequently in language, such as *is* and *the*), to be taught at each grade level. Often, high-frequency words do not have regular phonics patterns, and just have to be learned (e.g., *laugh, through, were*). We admit that this is more like a one-size-fits-all approach, but because it is embedded in writer's workshop and in the school's approach to spelling instruction, it seems to work. However, as with any one-size-fits-all approach, you have to have contingency plans for students who don't fit.

Mr. Porter uses his analysis of errors on writing samples to pick up on gaps in students' understandings of spelling patterns that were introduced in first grade and to pick up on the needs of advanced students. He uses small-group mini-lessons or writing conferences to teach children who were not in the typical range of achievement for the majority of the class.

Whole-Group Mini-Lesson

Here's an example of a whole-group mini-lesson on contractions. Mr. Porter wanted students to understand the concepts underlying contraction-making so that they would know where to put the apostrophe when they wrote contractions. He also wanted them to be able to figure out contractions in reading. A good way to study contractions is by families so students can see the pattern for making contractions.

Mr. Porter cleared the word wall of all other words in preparation for making a "contractions wall." He chose to work on contractions made with *'s* (*is, has*) and *'d* (*had, would*) in today's lesson, but he would cover other contraction patterns in lessons later in the week. Mr. Porter decided to use magnetic letters on the overhead to demonstrate how contractions are made because the magnetic letters provide a concrete example of the apostrophe that replaces letters. The lesson sequence went something like this:

- He began by giving the students a rationale for the lesson (so they would know how to make contractions in their writing).
- He assembled the words *he is* and *he had* with magnetic letters on the overhead.
- By manipulating the letters, he showed them how *he is* becomes *he's* by replacing the *i* in *is* with an apostrophe. He also gave them an example of a sentence with the contraction in it.
- He followed the same procedure with *he had* to form *he'd.*
- He left the two exemplars on the overhead with the missing letters in view above the contractions.
- He assembled *here is* and *I had* under the matching exemplars and asked students to come up and move the letters to form new contractions.
- He left these four exemplars on the overhead and assembled *she has* and *we would* under the *'s* and *'d* categories. He demonstrated how these words formed similar contractions and used them in a sentence.
- New words *where has* and *who would* went up on the screen. He invited another student to form new contractions with these.
- Finally, he and the students brainstormed other contractions made with *'s* and *'d* and Mr. Porter wrote them in under the appropriate categories to create two lists.
- Mr. Porter assigned each student to write one of the contractions and the two words that formed it on pieces of tag board with magic markers.
- He pinned the tag board under the *'d* (*had, would*) and *'s* (*is, has*) on the word wall, reminding the students, as they went off to get their writing portfolios, to try using contractions in their writing.

Mr. Porter approaches mini-lessons on other concepts for study in the second-grade curriculum in this way. His small-group mini-lessons are similar but involve just a few students with a similar instructional need. Small-group mini-lessons is one way to individualize instruction for students who have gaps in phonics concepts.

Accommodating Individual Differences

Sometimes students need instruction individualized just for them. Both writer's and reader's workshops provide contexts for individualized instruction.

Individualizing Instruction in Writer's Workshop

Writing conferences provide another context for individualizing instruction. Mr. Porter met with Michael for an individual conference on affricates, a concept usually learned at the letter-name stage. You read Michael's writing sample in Chapter 4. He substituted *chined* for *tried* in his story. Mr. Porter wasn't sure if Michael was having trouble with affricates or with consonant blends and digraphs in general. This seemed like a considerable gap for a student who was predicted to be at the transitional/within-word-pattern level, reading texts in the K range.

Mr. Porter began his writing conference by praising Michael's efforts on *The Singing Bone* (see Chapter 4), responding to the story as a reader. Then, he moved into the individual lesson focused on highlighting and comparing the sounds of consonant clusters *dr* and *tr* and the letter *j*. He sat beside Michael and used a small white board to demonstrate patterns in words, asking Michael to brainstorm words he knew that began with *dr, tr,* and *j*. Then, just to be sure, he reviewed with Michael the consonant digraphs *sh* and *ch* in the same way. Finally, Mr. Porter went back to Michael's story and helped him hear the *tr* at the beginning of *tried*.

Individualizing Instruction in Reader's Workshop

Toby is a student who's having extreme difficulty learning to read. He began the second grade reading at text level D (5/6). By the third month he was struggling with books at level E (7/8). Mr. Porter's statement about Toby's use of information on text reading on the Class Record Form (see Chapter 5) indicated that Toby was relying mainly on the initial letter as a phonics clue. This was corroborated by his performance on the Names Test—0 correct out of 70. We see a similar pattern on the writing and spelling assessments. Toby tended to represent just the beginning and ending sounds in writing words he did not know, and he was operating at the beginning of the letter-name stage of spelling development.

Mr. Porter decided to organize extra guided and explicit instruction for Toby. When it was appropriate, Toby sat in on guided reading phonics lessons with Alex, Maria, Spencer, Miranda, and Nathan. However, Mr. Porter also tried to provide Toby with both a shared reading lesson and a guided reading lesson each day. Many days Mr. Porter managed to squeeze a ten-minute one-on-one guided reading lesson out of the reader's workshop block. When Mr. Porter was working with small groups, Toby had independent activities suited to his development. For example, he kept a word study notebook, completed word sorts, and played phonics games as did other students, but the activities were designed just for him.

Linking Phonics Instruction with Content Area Study

Mr. Porter frequently links word study with content area units in science and social studies. This helps students realize that they can apply the word analysis skills they are learning in reading and writing in other contexts. In return, content area studies provide a rich source for both vocabulary development and extended word work. When Mr. Porter's students were studying amphibians in science, he used this opportunity to teach the concept that some parts of words in English are borrowed from other languages. Once you learn to recognize some word parts that turn up frequently in English, you can use this to decode unfamiliar words and to figure out what the words probably mean.

After the class was well immersed in its study of amphibians, Mr. Porter did a quick word study lesson at the beginning of a science class.

- Using the overhead projector, he asked the students to define the word *amphibian;* he wrote their definition on the transparency: "animals that are born in the water and later live on land."
- Then, Mr. Porter told the students that some words are made up of parts that you could use to figure out what a word means, even if you had never seen the word. He went on to explain that many words in science come from Greek roots, and knowing some of the Greek word parts and their meanings will help them figure out some new words in science.
- Mr. Porter wrote *amphibian* on the transparency and marked the parts of the word that are meaning units: *amphi/bi/an.*
- Mr. Porter then explained what each part meant: *amphi* - on both sides, *bi* - of living things (biological), and *an* - a common suffix meaning belonging to, born in, or living in. The class reconstructed a definition for *amphibian:* belonging to a group of living things that lives on both sides—water and land.

In this case, Mr. Porter was teaching morphology as well as phonics, but it is all part of word study in a well-integrated classroom.

A Summary of Principles

What makes phonics teaching systematic is knowing the concepts in the curriculum to teach, knowing whom to teach them to, having a plan to methodically teach concepts, and keeping records of learning and teaching in phonics. Here is a summary of principles for explicit, systematic phonics instruction in early literacy contexts that are outlined throughout this book.

Assessment and Record Keeping

Assessing what students know about phonics and having a reliable record of their changing knowledge at your fingertips are key to systematic instruction. Following are principles for assessing students' phonics knowledge in reading and writing and principles for record keeping.

Assessing Phonics in Reading

- Begin phonics assessment in reading by finding students' instructional text levels. Instructional text level is a good first indicator of a student's phase of phonics development.
- Analyze patterns of errors and self-corrections to home in on which phonics concepts students can use and which they need to be taught.
- Categorize students' errors on running records according to developmental phases. Focus on errors that indicate the student's estimated level of development and errors that are from an earlier phase. In general, ignore errors related to word patterns typically studied at more advanced stages.
- Assess phonemic awareness in preschool and kindergarten.
- Assess letter and letter-sound knowledge in kindergarten and first grade.
- Use the Names Test at the end of first grade and in second grade to assess how well students can use phonics concepts to decode unfamiliar words without context cues.

115

- Assess phonics learning in both reading and writing contexts, because students may not fit neatly into one phase of development in both reading and writing.

Assessing Phonics in Writing

- Analyze students' errors in writing samples and on a developmental spelling test to identify gaps in learning or to discover which concepts within the phase need to be covered.
- Analyze writing samples both to determine the percentage of conventional spelling used and to categorize errors according to the developmental phases. The quantitative and qualitative analyses provide rough benchmarks of change over time. For example, a student who consistently misspells 50 percent of the words in writing samples taken over time may not be making much progress with using phonics in writing. Conversely, a student who moves from making many errors in the letter-name category to making very few errors in the letter-name category is likely making progress in using phonics in writing.

Record Keeping

- Have at your fingertips what the students know in order to teach them what they do not yet know. Keeping records of assessment findings is key to teaching systematically.
- Keep records of individual student work, like running records and writing samples, in order to plan instruction for individuals.
- Keep records of reading and spelling development for your class as a whole in order to group students for instruction.
- Keep records of individual student achievement over time in order to talk with parents, administrators, or the school literacy team (e.g., classroom teachers, special educators, literacy specialists, Title I tutors) about student progress or lack of progress in phonics.
- Keep records of what you taught and whom you taught it to so that no students fall between the cracks in phonics instruction.

Curriculum and Instruction

Knowing the phonics elements to teach and using a variety of early literacy contexts in which to teach them are the keys to explicit instruction. Following are principles to guide curricular and instructional decisions.

- Match instruction to students, based on assessment and the curriculum.
- Assume that most of the students at a particular grade level need to be taught how to use the phonics concepts in writing that are outlined in the curriculum for that grade level. However, use assessment information to home in on exactly what concepts in a phase students need to learn.
- Teach phonics concepts in reading guided by students' instructional text level and an analysis of running record errors. Phonics development may be different in reading and writing.
- Teach from a curriculum that is based on the ways students typically develop phonics knowledge in reading and writing.
- Teach for phonics *concepts* (i.e., patterns for how words work) and the item learning will follow. For example, if you want to teach children about *ed* and *ing,* teach the concept that endings can be added to a familiar word to make a new word. *Ed, ing, s, er,* and *est* are endings that can be added to words; they are the *items.*
- Teach phonics concepts within each developmental phase in the curriculum in any sequence, depending on the needs of the learners and the texts they are reading and writing.
- Teach phonics concepts from an earlier phase if students have gaps in understanding, even if they demonstrate use of some concepts at a more advanced phase. Don't assume students will just "get it."
- Teach in a way that fosters students' natural ability to notice phonics patterns because the human brain is a pattern detector, not a rule applier.
- Use words the students know to teach concepts. It is hard for students to learn something new if they have no "hooks" on which to hang the new learning. For example, in preschool and kindergarten, begin teaching letter names and sounds using children's names. In first grade, if you want to teach students about the *ook* phonics pattern, use simple words they can already read or write (e.g., *look* and *book*) to teach the concept. Then, present a new word, like *snooker,* and provide assistance as the students use their new knowledge to figure out the longer, more complicated word.
- Teach phonics in a variety of literacy and content contexts to ensure students transfer phonics knowledge to real reading and writing tasks.
- Teach for and assess *both* what students know about phonics *and* how they can use it in reading and writing contexts.
- Teach phonemic awareness in preschool and kindergarten and then move on to phonics.

- Teach letter recognition, naming, and formation in preschool and kindergarten. Knowing how to distinguish one letter from another is as powerful an indicator of early reading success as phonemic awareness. Success in phonics learning depends on letter knowledge.

Throughout this book we have made the point that phonics can be taught systematically and explicitly across the literacy block and in the content areas. A one-size-fits-all phonics program does not make sense, because students have difficulty transferring decontextualized learning to real reading and writing tasks. In addition, as students gain experience with reading and writing, their knowledge of phonics in reading and writing may begin to differ. With phonics instruction embedded in many instructional contexts, students easily learn phonics and how to use phonics for many purposes; they begin to recognize and use the systematic sound systems in many words they want to read and write.

Key Concepts to Teach at Different Grade Levels

Preschool

Emergent/Prephonemic Stage

Students at this level are typically in preschool. They are exploring the sounds of language (phonological and phonemic awareness) with songs, rhymes, games, and big-book shared reading experiences. They are also learning letter names at the same time they are learning how books work—that pages are turned left to right, there is a beginning and an end to a book, and that print (not pictures) tells the story. Typically, in preschool children are also beginning a long journey in learning to perceive similarities and differences in letters; this ability to visually discriminate between letters is as important in learning to read as learning to aurally discriminate between sounds. Key concepts for you to know when teaching children at this level include the following.

Phonological Awareness
- Language is made up of sounds.
- If you listen closely, you can hear those sounds.
- There are sounds that are the same and sounds that are different.

Phonemic Awareness
- Words are made up of individual sounds that are blended (e.g., /c/+/a/+/t/ = *cat*).
- You can hear all the individual sounds in words.
- You can change those sounds to change the word (e.g., change the /c/ in *cat* to /h/ and you change the word to *hat*).

Visual Perception of Letters
- Writing is made up of letters and spaces.
- You have to look carefully at letters to see how they are alike and different (e.g., tall, short, made with circles, sticks, and half-circles).

Kindergarten

Emergent/Letter-Name Stage

Students at the emergent/letter-name stage are typically in kindergarten. They know how books work and they are now learning how print works—spoken words match one-to-one with printed words when reading and writing. They are also refining their knowledge of letters through instruction in letter formation and letter-sound match. Key concepts for you to know when teaching children at this level include the following.

Initial Consonants
- Words are made up of letters.
- Letters have names.
- Letters give words their sounds.
- The sound of the first letter in a word you don't know helps you figure out what the word is—if you also check that it makes sense.
- Letters are formed in particular ways that make them easier to make.
- If you practice making letters so that you can make them easily and quickly, it makes writing stories easier.
- Neat and well-formed letters are easier to read than poorly formed letters.

Word Knowledge
- Names are words that you can learn and recognize immediately.
- Words in reading are the same as words in writing (and vice versa).
- You can learn to recognize some words "by sight," and that makes reading faster and easier.
- You can learn to write some words without needing to think about the letters and sounds, and that makes writing faster and easier.

Grade One

Early/Letter-Name Stage

Early/letter-name readers and writers are typically at the end of kindergarten or beginning of first grade. They have developed phonemic awareness and are able to name many letters and letter sounds. They are ready to learn much more about consonant sounds: final consonant sounds, initial and final consonant blends, and initial and final consonant digraphs. They are also ready to begin exploring short vowels, word families, and those tricky affricative consonants. Key concepts for you to know when teaching students at this level include the following.

More About Consonants
- Consonants are all the letters in the alphabet except *a, e, i, o,* and *u.* *Y* is sometimes a consonant (e.g., *yes, yellow,* and *yokes*).
- You can check for letter sounds at the ends of words to help you figure out words you don't know.
- Two or more consonants (e.g., *bl, st,* and *cr*) can come together at the beginning or ends of words to make a blended sound.
- Sometimes two consonants come together to make one sound that is different from either of the letter's own sounds (e.g., **sh**oe, **t**oo**th**, **ch**ur**ch**, *and* **wh**en).

Short Vowels
- *A, e, i, o, u,* and sometimes *y* are vowels. Vowels are letters that can make a variety of sounds, depending on the letters around them.
- A pattern of consonant-vowel-consonant (CVC) usually gives a vowel its "short" sound (e.g., *cat, get, pin, top,* and *but*).

Word Families with Short Vowels
- Words that look alike at the end often rhyme (e.g., *cat* and *hat*).
- Knowing the rhyming part of one word can help you figure out other words that look like it.
- You can change the letter or letters in front of a rhyming pattern to make new words (e.g., change the *c* in *cat* to *fl* and you have *flat*).

Inflected Endings
- You can take a word you know and change it by adding an ending in writing (e.g., *cat/cats, help/helping,* and *kick/kicked*).
- You can look for familiar endings on words to help you figure out words in reading.

Early/Within-Word-Pattern Stage

At some point in first grade, early readers typically are ready for more complex phonics instruction because the books they are reading increase in length, and words become more difficult to "sound out." Early/within-word-pattern learners are ready to learn about long vowel patterns, *r*-controlled vowels, and complex consonant clusters. Key concepts for you to know when teaching students at this level include the following.

Long Vowels
- A pattern of vowel-consonant-*e* (VCe) in a word usually means the first vowel says its long sound and the *e* is silent (e.g., *cake, kite,* and *hope*).

- A pattern of consonant-vowel-vowel-consonant (CVVC) usually means the first vowel says its long sound and the other vowel is "silent" (e.g., *rain, meat,* and *cue*).
- Knowing the vowel pattern in one word can help you figure out other words with that pattern.

R-Controlled Vowels

- *R* after a vowel changes its sound (e.g., *car, her, fur, ear,* and *hair*).
- Because *ir, er,* and *ur* represent the same sound at times you just have to remember how /er/ is spelled in particular words in order to write them correctly.
- Knowing the *r*-controlled pattern in one word can help you figure out other words with that pattern in reading.

More About Consonants

- *C* sounds like /s/ and *g* often sounds like /j/ when *e, i,* or *y* come after them (e.g., *city* and *cage*).
- *Get* and *give* are exceptions to this pattern.
- Knowing common vowel patterns with soft *c* and *g* (e.g., *ace* and *age*) can help you figure out other words with that pattern.
- Some consonants don't make a sound in some words (e.g., *night* and *comb*).
- Knowing common letter patterns that contain silent letters can help you figure out other words with that pattern.
- Three consonants coming together at the beginning or end of a word make up a common letter pattern (e.g., *scramble, ditch,* and *through*).
- Knowing those common patterns with three consonants can help you figure out other words with that pattern.

Grade Two

Transitional/Within-Word-Pattern Stage

Transitional readers who are within-word-pattern spellers are typically at the end of first grade or into second grade. They are learning about nontypical, or abstract, vowel patterns such as *au, ow,* and *oi.* They are also learning about the different sounds that the inflected ending *ed* can make. Knowing about homophones, homographs, and contractions is also useful for learners at this phase of development. Key concepts for you to know when teaching students at this level include the following.

Abstract Vowels

- *Oo* (*book*), *oo* (*boot*) *ou, au, ui, ow, aw, oi/oy* and *al* make sounds that differ from either the long or short sound of the vowels.
- Knowing words with those unusual vowels (e.g., *mall, out, saw,* and *boy*) can help you figure out other words with the same pattern.

Sounds for *-ed*

- Regardless of how it is pronounced, *-ed* is used to indicate an event that happened in the past.
- /ed/ can be pronounced three ways: /id/, /d/, or /t/.

Homophones

- Some words sound alike but have different spellings and meanings (e.g., *pair/pear* and *meat/meet*).
- You have to pay attention to remember and use the correct spelling of homophones in writing.

Homographs

- Some words look alike but have different pronunciations and meanings, for example, "Today I will *read* the paper at breakfast, but yesterday I *read* the paper after dinner."
- In reading, the context helps you know which pronunciation to give the word.

Contractions

- Two words can be combined to make one shorter word that means the same (e.g., *I am* becomes *I'm*).
- When combining two words into a shorter word, you leave out some letters and put in an apostrophe; it marks the spot where letters were taken out.
- Knowing some contractions helps you figure out other contractions that are made the same way.

Transitional/Syllable-Juncture Stage

Transitional readers who are spelling at the syllable-juncture stage are typically in second grade and reading texts with more sophisticated vocabulary and more complex spelling patterns. They have mastered patterns in single-syllable words and are now learning more about how patterns apply to polysyllabic words. The concepts they are working on include compound words, doubling consonants and dropping *e* with *ed* and *ing* endings, and how syllable juncture (i.e., where one syllable begins and another ends) is a clue to syllable pronunciation in reading, and how pronunciation is a clue to syllable juncture in writing. Key concepts for you to know when teaching students at this level include the following.

Syllables

- All syllables are marked by a "beat." For example, *help* has one beat, *helpful* has two beats, and *helpfully* has three beats.
- All syllables have at least one vowel and may or may not have consonants (e.g., the first syllable in *awake* has no consonants).

Open and Closed Syllables

- Where one syllable begins and another ends is called the syllable juncture.
- The vowel pattern at this juncture usually determines the sound of the vowel in the first syllable. VCC•VC as in *help•er* or VC•CV as in *tem•per* marks a closed or short vowel in the first syllable. V•CV as in *rea•son* marks an open or long vowel in the first syllable.
- You can usually use the vowel and consonant patterns at syllable juncture to pronounce words in reading and write words you don't know how to spell.
- Not all words follow the rules; in reading, you have to try pronouncing unknown words several ways to figure out a word that makes sense in the context.

Stressed Syllables

- One syllable usually has more emphasis, or stress, than the others.
- The stressed syllable often has a long vowel sound.
- In two-syllable words, the first syllable is usually accented or stressed.
- Prefixes and suffixes are rarely stressed (*un•HAPPY, MAIN•ly*).
- To figure out an unknown word in reading it is helpful to try putting the stress on different syllables until you find a word that makes sense in the context.
- It is helpful to use the vowel patterns and stress patterns in words you know to figure out words that are new to you.

Compound Words

- Compound words can be formed by combining two smaller words.
- In reading, you can figure out compound words by looking for the two smaller words at the syllable juncture.
- In writing you have to use the context to know which words can be formed into compound words, and which cannot. Often, words that can be formed into compound words are "describing words" (i.e., adjectives) (e.g., The girl had a *red-haired* brother, or Her brother had *red hair.*)

Doubling Consonants

- When adding *ed* or *ing* or other endings that begin with a vowel to words with short vowels, you usually double the final consonant in writing (e.g., *pet/petted*).
- If you are trying to figure out a word with an ending in reading, it is helpful to find the base word, recognizing that an extra consonant may have been added (e.g., **stop***ping*).

Dropping *e*

- When adding *ed* or *ing* or other endings that begin with a vowel to words that end with *e*, you usually drop the *e* in writing (e.g., *like/liking*).
- If you are trying to figure out a word with an ending in reading, it is helpful to find the base word, recognizing that an *e* may have been dropped.

Plurals

- You add *s* to the ends of many nouns without making any changes to the word (e.g., *cats* and *dogs*).
- You add *es* to words that end in *s* (*buses*), *x* (*boxes*), *sh* (*brushes*), and *ch* (*churches*).
- In words that end in a consonant and *y*, change the *y* to *i* (*fly/flies*), and in words that end in a vowel and *y*, just add *s* (*turkey/turkeys*).
- There are exceptions that you just have to learn (e.g., *eat/ate*, *tooth/teeth*, *half/halves*, and *deer/deer*).

Possessives

- When nouns don't end in *s*, you add an apostrophe *s* to show ownership (e.g., *boy/boy's*, *mouse/mouse's*, and *children/children's*).
- For plural nouns that end in *s*, just add an apostrophe after the *s* (e.g., *dogs/dogs'* and *boys/boys'*).

Affixes

- Prefixes and suffixes change the meaning of a base word, so you need to know what the prefixes and suffixes mean (e.g., *agree* and *disagree*).
- Suffixes that begin with a vowel, like *er*, usually require doubling the final consonant, dropping the *e*, or changing *y* to *i* on a base word (e.g., *bigger*, *bluer*, and *funnier*).
- Suffixes that begin with a consonant rarely require changing the base word (e.g., *care**ful***).

Analysis of Errors on Running Records
Emergent and Early/Letter-Name Development Stages (K–1)

Student _____ Date _____

Book _____ Text Level _____

Categories of Error	**Student's Error/Word in Text**

Initial Consonants
(e.g., <u>b</u>all, <u>l</u>ike, <u>m</u>e)

_____

Final Consonants
(e.g., go<u>t</u>, bal<u>l</u>, slee<u>p</u>)

_____

Initial Consonant Blends
(e.g., <u>st</u>op, <u>pl</u>ease, <u>bl</u>ack)

_____

Initial Consonant Digraphs
(e.g., <u>sh</u>eep, <u>ch</u>ip, <u>th</u>is, <u>wh</u>en)

_____

Short Vowels/Word Families
(e.g., b<u>ad</u>, l<u>et</u>, d<u>ig</u>)

_____

Inflected Endings
(e.g., go<u>ing</u>, kick<u>ed</u>)

_____

Final Consonant Blends
(e.g., he<u>lp</u>, du<u>mp</u>, po<u>nd</u>)

_____

Final Consonant Digraphs
(e.g., mu<u>ch</u>, fi<u>sh</u>, ma<u>th</u>)

Sound Systems: Explicit, Systematic Phonics in Early Literacy Contexts by Anna Lyon and Paula Moore. Copyright © 2003. Stenhouse Publishers.

Analysis of Errors on Running Records
Early/Within-Word-Pattern and Transitional/Within-Word-Pattern Stages

Student _____ Date _____

Book _____ Text Level _____

Categories of Error	Student's Error/Word in Text
VCe Vowel Patterns (e.g., b<u>ake</u>, k<u>ite</u>, h<u>ole</u>)	
CVVC Vowel Patterns (e.g., r<u>ain</u>, sh<u>eep</u>, c<u>oat</u>)	
Other Long Vowel Patterns (e.g., n<u>ight</u>, c<u>old</u>, bl<u>ue</u>, m<u>ay</u>)	
R-controlled Vowel Patterns (e.g., c<u>ar</u>, h<u>er</u>, f<u>ir</u>, f<u>or</u>, f<u>ur</u>)	
Abstract Vowel Patterns (e.g., b<u>oy</u>, b<u>ook</u>, cl<u>own</u>)	
Complex Consonant Blends (e.g., <u>qu</u>iet, <u>scr</u>am, <u>thr</u>ew)	
Hard and Soft c & g (e.g., cell/call, rag/rage)	
Silent Consonants (e.g., com<u>b</u>, <u>w</u>rite, <u>k</u>now)	
Sounds for *ed* (e.g., lifted, rained, asked)	
Homophones (e.g., their/there, hear/here)	
Homographs (e.g., read/read)	
Contractions (e.g., you're, she'd, let's)	

Analysis of Errors on Running Records
Transitional/Syllable-Juncture Stage

Student _____   Date _____
Book _____   Text Level _____

Categories of Error	Student's Error/Word in Text

Compound Words
(e.g., bookcase, twenty-five)

_____

Doubling Consonant
(e.g., bat/batted)

_____

Dropping *e*
(e.g., hope/hoping)

_____

Open Syllable Patterns
(e.g., pi•rate, o•pen, rea•son)

_____

Closed Syllable Patterns
(e.g., en•ter, bas•ket, but•ter)

_____

Syllable Stress
(e.g., un•HAPPY, MAIN•ly)

_____

Plurals
(e.g., dog<u>s</u>, beach<u>es</u>, pon<u>ies</u>)

_____

Possessives
(e.g., boy's/boys')

_____

Prefixes
(e.g., <u>dis</u>like, <u>mis</u>fit, <u>re</u>fill)

_____

Suffixes
(e.g., cheer<u>ful</u>, like<u>ly</u>, sick<u>ness</u>)

Sound Systems: Explicit, Systematic Phonics in Early Literacy Contexts by Anna Lyon and Paula Moore. Copyright © 2003. Stenhouse Publishers.

Dynamic Assessment of Phonemic Awareness

Developed by Janet E. Spector
College of Education and Human Development
University of Maine

Overview

The Dynamic Assessment of Phonemic Awareness is an informal measure of sensitivity to the sound structure of words. It is designed to be used with children between the ages of 3 and 8 years. The procedure uses corrective feedback and increasingly supportive prompts and cues when a child is unable to segment a word correctly. The tester uses the following series of prompts each time a child is unable to segment a word:

(1) pronounce the target word slowly
(2) ask the child to identify the first sound of the word
(3) cue the child with the first sound
(4) cue the child with the number of sounds
(5) model segmentation using pennies placed in squares to represent the number of sounds in the word
(6) model segmentation as above, but working hand-over-hand with the child while placing pennies in squares
(7) repeat prompt 6

The task comprises twelve items: four CV words (i.e., *say, pie, we, two*), four VC words (i.e., *age, eat, egg, if*), and four CVC words (i.e., *leg, feet, page, rice*). These words were selected both because they were

Spector, J. E. 1997. Dynamic Assessment of Phonemic Awareness. (CD-ROM). (Online). Abstracts from Knowledge Access, OVID Technologies. HaPI item: 15521.

expected to be familiar to young children and because they include a range of vowel and consonant sounds.

Introductory Instructions to Students

"Now we are going to play a game with sounds. I will say a word and ask you to break the word apart. You will have to tell me each sound that you hear in the word. For example, if I say 'old,' you will say 'o-l-d.' Let's try a few more."

General Procedures

Begin with item 1 on the response sheet ("say") and continue through item 12. Whenever a child is unable to segment a word correctly, move the child through the prompts (in order) until he or she produces the correct segmentation. For example, if on item 4, the child achieves success on prompt 2, move next to item 5. If the child cannot segment item 5 on the first attempt, move the child through the prompts again, beginning with prompt 1. Discontinue testing after the first two items if a child does not achieve success in segmenting on either item 1 or 2. Remember, a child is considered successful if he or she responds correctly to any of the prompts (including the three prompts that require imitation only).

Prompts

P1: "Listen while I say the word very slowly." Model slow pronunciation. "Now can you tell me each sound?"

P2: "What's the first sound you hear in _____ ?" If first sound is correct: "Now can you tell me each of the sounds?" If incorrect or no response: "Try to tell me just a little bit of the word." If child still does not isolate first sound, skip P3 and P4. Go to P5.

P3: If child correctly identified first sound, but not next sound(s): "___ is the first sound in ___. What sound comes next? Now can you tell me each sound?"

P4: "There are two (three) sounds in _____. What are they?"

P5: "Watch me." Model segmentation of word: Place a token in a square as each sound is spoken, then repeat word as a whole. After demo say: "Try to do what I just did." Score response as correct if child can imitate correct segmentation.

I1: "Let's try it together." Model segmentation of word with child. Work hand-over-hand with child and ask child to pronounce segments along with you. "Now try to do it yourself. Do what we just did together."

I2: Model again with child. "Now try again to do it yourself."

Scoring

Performance on dynamic phoneme segmentation indicates the degree of independence that the child achieves in performing the segmentation task. If desired, each item can be scored as follows:

6 = correct response with no prompts required
5 = correct response after prompt 1
4 = correct response after prompt 2
3 = correct response after prompt 3
2 = correct response after prompt 4
1 = correct response after prompt 5
0 = no correct response

Performance on the last two imitation trials (i.e., I1 and I2) does not contribute to scores.

Response Sheet

Name:

Date:

Part 1 (CV words)	Part 2 (VC words)	Part 3 (CVC words)

1. say _____

P1 (slowly) _____
P2 (first sound) _____
P3 (next sound) _____
P4 (2 sounds) _____
P5 (demo) _____
I1 _____
I2 _____

5. age _____

P1 (slowly) _____
P2 (first sound) _____
P3 (next sound) _____
P4 (2 sounds) _____
P5 (demo) _____
I1 _____
I2 _____

9. leg _____

P1 (slowly) _____
P2 (first sound) _____
P3 (next sound) _____
P4 (2 sounds) _____
P5 (demo) _____
I1 _____
I2 _____

2. pie _____

P1 (slowly) _____
P2 (first sound) _____
P3 (next sound) _____
P4 (2 sounds) _____
P5 (demo) _____
I1 _____
I2 _____

6. eat _____

P1 (slowly) _____
P2 (first sound) _____
P3 (next sound) _____
P4 (2 sounds) _____
P5 (demo) _____
I1 _____
I2 _____

10. feet _____

P1 (slowly) _____
P2 (first sound) _____
P3 (next sound) _____
P4 (2 sounds) _____
P5 (demo) _____
I1 _____
I2 _____

3. we _____
P1 (slowly) _____
P2 (first sound) _____
P3 (next sound) _____
P4 (2 sounds) _____
P5 (demo) _____
I1 _____
I2 _____

7. egg _____
P1 (slowly) _____
P2 (first sound) _____
P3 (next sound) _____
P4 (2 sounds) _____
P5 (demo) _____
I1 _____
I2 _____

11. page _____
P1 (slowly) _____
P2 (first sound) _____
P3 (next sound) _____
P4 (2 sounds) _____
P5 (demo) _____
I1 _____
I2 _____

4. two _____
P1 (slowly) _____
P2 (first sound) _____
P3 (next sound) _____
P4 (2 sounds) _____
P5 (demo) _____
I1 _____
I2 _____

8. if _____
P1 (slowly) _____
P2 (first sound) _____
P3 (next sound) _____
P4 (2 sounds) _____
P5 (demo) _____
I1 _____
I2 _____

12. rice _____
P1 (slowly) _____
P2 (first sound) _____
P3 (next sound) _____
P4 (2 sounds) _____
P5 (demo) _____
I1 _____
I2 _____

Administering, Scoring, and Interpreting Errors on the Names Test

Administering the Names Test

1. Administer the Names Test individually in a quiet, distraction-free location.
2. Explain to the student that she or he is to pretend to be a teacher who must read a list of names of students in the class. Direct the student to read the names as if taking attendance.
3. Have the student read the entire list. Inform the student that you will not be able to help with difficult names, and encourage him or her to "make a guess if you are not sure." This way you will have sufficient responses for analysis.
4. Write a check on the scoring sheet for each name read correctly. Write phonetic spellings for names that are mispronounced.

Scoring Errors on the Names Test

1. Count a word correct if all syllables are pronounced correctly regardless of where the student places the accent. For example, either Yo'/lan/da or Yo/lan'/da would be acceptable.
2. For words where the vowel pronunciation depends on which syllable the consonant is placed with, count them correct for either pronunciation. For example, Ho/mer or Hom/er would be acceptable.
3. Count the number of names read correctly, and analyze those mispronounced, looking for patterns indicative of decoding strengths and weaknesses.

Analyzing Errors on the Names Test

1. Make a copy of the Matrix for Analyzing Errors on the Names Test for each student.
2. Locate the name that the student misread in the lefthand column.

Circle the phonics element in the name that the student misread. For example, if the student read Jenny for Gene, you would circle the *ene*. The soft *g* was pronounced correctly so you would not circle the *g*.

3. Note the categories in which the student makes the most errors. These are phonics generalizations that may need to be explicitly taught in reading instruction.

4. Fill in the Class Record Sheet for Names Test to look for patterns in missed phonics elements to group students for explicit instruction.

Phonics Categories for Analyzing Errors

The following abbreviations for phonics categories are used on the Matrix for Analyzing Errors on the Names Test, as well as on the Class Record Sheet.

Phonics Category	Instances
Initial consonants (InCon)	37
Initial consonant blends (InConBl)	19
Consonant digraphs (ConDgr)	15
Short vowels (ShVow)	36
Long vowels/VC-final *e* (LV/VC-e)	23
Vowel digraphs (VowDgr)	15
Controlled vowels (CtVow)	25
Schwa	(15)

Names Test of Decoding
Student's Copy

Directions: Pretend you are a teacher who is taking attendance on the first day of school. Please read your new students' names from the list.

Jay Conway	Dee Skidmore
Tim Cornell	Grace Brewster
Chuck Hoke	Ned Westmorland
Yolanda Clark	Ron Smitherman
Kimberly Blake	Troy Whitlock
Roberta Slade	Vance Middleton
Homer Preston	Zane Anderson
Gus Quincy	Shane Fletcher
Cindy Sampson	Floyd Sheldon
Chester Wright	Dean Bateman
Ginger Yale	Thelma Rinehart
Patrick Tweed	Austin Shepherd
Stanley Shaw	Bertha Dale
Wendy Swain	Neal Wade
Glen Spencer	Jake Murphy
Fred Sherwood	Joan Brooks
Flo Thornton	Gene Loomis
Bernard Pendergraph	

Names Test of Decoding
Scoring Sheet

Child's Name: _____   Teacher's Name: _____

School: _____   Grade: _____   Date: _____

1. _____ Jay Conway	2. _____ Tim Cornell	3. _____ Chuck Hoke	4. _____ Yolanda Clark
5. _____ Kimberly Blake	6. _____ Roberta Slade	7. _____ Homer Preston	8. _____ Gus Quincy
9. _____ Cindy Sampson	10. _____ Chester Wright	11. _____ Ginger Yale	12. _____ Patrick Tweed
13. _____ Stanley Shaw	14. _____ Wendy Swain	15. _____ Glen Spencer	16. _____ Fred Sherwood
17. _____ Flo Thornton	18. _____ Bernard Pendergraph	19. _____ Dee Skidmore	20. _____ Grace Brewster
21. _____ Ned Westmorland	22. _____ Ron Smitherman	23. _____ Troy Whitlock	24. _____ Vance Middleton
25. _____ Zane Anderson	26. _____ Shane Fletcher	27. _____ Floyd Sheldon	28. _____ Dean Bateman
29. _____ Thelma Rinehart	30. _____ Austin Shepherd	31. _____ Bertha Dale	32. _____ Neal Wade
33. _____ Jake Murphy	34. _____ Joan Brooks	35. _____ Gene Loomis	

FINAL SCORE: _____ /70

(ONE POINT FOR EACH FIRST NAME AND ONE POINT FOR EACH LAST NAME CORRECT)

Duffelmeyer, F. A., A. E. Kruse, D. J. Merkley, and S. A. Fyfe. 1994. "Further Validation and Enhancements of the Names Test." *Reading Teacher* 48: 118–128.

Matrix for Analyzing Errors on the Names Test

Name _____ Date _____

Name	InCon	InConBl	ConDgr	ShVow	LV/VC-e	VowDgr	CtVow	Schwa
Anderson				A			er	o
Austin						Au		i
Bateman	B				ate			a
Bernard	B						er, ar	
Bertha	B		th				er	a
Blake		Bl			ake			
Brewster		Br					ew, er	
Brooks		Br				oo		
Chester			Ch	e			er	
Chuck			Ch	u				
Cindy	C			i	y			
Clark		Cl					ar	
Conway	C			o		ay		
Cornell	C			e			or	
Dale	D				ale			
Dean	D					ea		
Dee	D					ee		
Fletcher		Fl	ch	e			er	
Flo		Fl			o			
Floyd		Fl				oy		
Fred		Fr		e				
Gene	G				ene			
Ginger	G			i			er	
Glen		Gl		e				
Grace		Gr			ace			
Gus	G			u		'		
Hoke	H				oke			
Homer	H				o		er	
Jake	J				ake			
Jay	J					ay		
Joan	J					oa		
Kimberly	K			i	y		er	
Loomis	L					oo		i
Middleton	M			i				o
Murphy	M		ph		y		ur	

Matrix for Analyzing Errors on the Names Test (cont.)

Name _____   Date _____

Name	InCon	InConBl	ConDgr	ShVow	LV/VC-e	VowDgr	CtVow	Schwa
Neal	N				ea			
Ned	N			e				
Patrick	P			a, i				
Pendergraph	P		ph	e, a			er	
Preston		Pr		e				o
Quincy				i	y			
Rinehart	R				ine		ar	
Roberta	R				o		er	a
Ron	R			o				
Sampson	S			a				o
Shane			Sh		ane			
Shaw			Sh				aw	
Sheldon			Sh	e				o
Shepherd			Sh	e			er	
Sherwood			Sh			oo	er	
Skidmore		Sk		i			or	
Slad		Sl			ade			
Smitherman		Sm	th	i			er	a
Spencer		Sp		e			er	
Stanley		St		a		ey		
Swain		Sw				ai		
Thelma			Th	e				a
Thornton			Th				or	o
Tim	T			i				
Troy		Tr				oy		
Tweed		Tw				ee		
Vance	V			a				
Wade	W				ade			
Wendy	W			e	y			
Westmoreland	W			e			or	a
Whitlock			Wh	i, o				
Wright					i			
Yale	Y				ale			
Yolanda	Y			a	o			a
Zane	Z				ane			

Sound Systems: Explicit, Systematic Phonics in Early Literacy Contexts by Anna Lyon and Paula Moore. Copyright © 2003. Stenhouse Publishers.

Class Record Sheet for Names Test

Directions: In each category, list the specific phonics elements your students were unable to decode. Group students for instruction based on common needs.

Student's Name	InCon	InConBl	ConDgr	ShVow	LV/VC-e	VowDgr	CtVow	Schwa

Analysis of Errors in Writing Samples
Emergent and Early/Letter-Name Development Stages (K–1)

Student _____ Date _____

Categories of Error   **Student's Error/Correct Spelling**

Initial Consonants
(e.g., <u>b</u>all, <u>l</u>ike, <u>m</u>e)

_____

Final Consonants
(e.g., go<u>t</u>, bal<u>l</u>, slee<u>p</u>)

_____

Initial Consonant Blends
(e.g., <u>st</u>op, <u>pl</u>ease, <u>bl</u>ack)

_____

Initial Consonant Digraphs
(e.g., <u>sh</u>eep, <u>ch</u>ip, <u>th</u>is, <u>wh</u>en)

_____

Short Vowels/Word Families
(e.g., b<u>a</u>d, l<u>e</u>t, d<u>i</u>g)

_____

Inflected Endings
(e.g., go<u>ing</u>, kick<u>ed</u>)

_____

Final Consonant Blends
(e.g., he<u>lp</u>, du<u>mp</u>, po<u>nd</u>)

_____

Final Consonant Digraphs
(e.g., mu<u>ch</u>, fi<u>sh</u>, ma<u>th</u>)

Sound Systems: Explicit, Systematic Phonics in Early Literacy Contexts by Anna Lyon and Paula Moore. Copyright © 2003. Stenhouse Publishers.

Analysis of Errors in Writing Samples
Early/Within-Word-Pattern and Transitional/Within-Word-Pattern Stages

Student_____ Date_____

Categories of Error	**Student's Error/Correct Spelling**
VCe Vowel Patterns (e.g., <u>ba</u>ke, <u>ki</u>te, h<u>ole</u>)	
CVVC Vowel Patterns (e.g., r<u>ain</u>, sh<u>ee</u>p, c<u>oa</u>t)	
Other Long Vowel Patterns (e.g., n<u>igh</u>t, c<u>old</u>, bl<u>ue</u>, m<u>ay</u>)	
R-controlled Vowel Patterns (e.g., c<u>ar</u>, h<u>er</u>, f<u>ir</u>, f<u>or</u>, f<u>ur</u>)	
Abstract Vowel Patterns (e.g., b<u>oy</u>, b<u>ook</u>, cl<u>own</u>)	
Complex Consonant Blends (e.g., <u>qu</u>iet, <u>scr</u>am, <u>thr</u>ew)	
Hard and Soft c & g (e.g., cell/call, rag/rage)	
Silent Consonants (e.g., com<u>b</u>, <u>wr</u>ite, <u>k</u>now)	
Sounds for *ed* (e.g., lifted, rained, asked)	
Homophones (e.g., their/there, hear/here)	
Homographs (e.g., read/read)	
Contractions (e.g., you're, she'd, let's)	

Analysis of Errors in Writing Samples
Transitional/Syllable-Juncture Stage

Student _____ Date _____

Categories of Error   **Student's Error/Correct Spelling**

Compound Words
(e.g., bookcase, twenty-five)

_____

Doubling Consonant
(e.g., bat/batted)

_____

Dropping *e*
(e.g., hope/hoping)

_____

Open Syllable Patterns
(e.g., pi•rate, o•pen, rea•son)

_____

Closed Syllable Patterns
(e.g., en•ter, bas•ket, but•ter)

_____

Syllable Stress
(e.g., un•HAPPY, MAIN•ly)

_____

Plurals
(e.g., dog<u>s</u>, beach<u>es</u>, pon<u>ies</u>)

_____

Possessives
(e.g., boy's/boys')

_____

Prefixes
(e.g., <u>dis</u>like, <u>mis</u>fit, <u>re</u>fill)

_____

Suffixes
(e.g., cheer<u>ful</u>, like<u>ly</u>, sick<u>ness</u>)

Class Knowledge of Letters and Letter Sounds

Grade: _____

Date: _____

Name	# Letters Known	Letters Unknown/Confused	# Sounds Known	Sounds Unknown/Confused
	Upper ____ / 26 Lower ____ / 26		Upper ____ / 26 Lower ____ / 26	
	Upper ____ / 26 Lower ____ / 26		Upper ____ / 26 Lower ____ / 26	
	Upper ____ / 26 Lower ____ / 26		Upper ____ / 26 Lower ____ / 26	
	Upper ____ / 26 Lower ____ / 26		Upper ____ / 26 Lower ____ / 26	
	Upper ____ / 26 Lower ____ / 26		Upper ____ / 26 Lower ____ / 26	
	Upper ____ / 26 Lower ____ / 26		Upper ____ / 26 Lower ____ / 26	
	Upper ____ / 26 Lower ____ / 26		Upper ____ / 26 Lower ____ / 26	
	Upper ____ / 26 Lower ____ / 26		Upper ____ / 26 Lower ____ / 26	
	Upper ____ / 26 Lower ____ / 26		Upper ____ / 26 Lower ____ / 26	
	Upper ____ / 26 Lower ____ / 26		Upper ____ / 26 Lower ____ / 26	
	Upper ____ / 26 Lower ____ / 26		Upper ____ / 26 Lower ____ / 26	
	Upper ____ / 26 Lower ____ / 26		Upper ____ / 26 Lower ____ / 26	
	Upper ____ / 26 Lower ____ / 26		Upper ____ / 26 Lower ____ / 26	
	Upper ____ / 26 Lower ____ / 26		Upper ____ / 26 Lower ____ / 26	
	Upper ____ / 26 Lower ____ / 26		Upper ____ / 26 Lower ____ / 26	
	Upper ____ / 26 Lower ____ / 26		Upper ____ / 26 Lower ____ / 26	
	Upper ____ / 26 Lower ____ / 26		Upper ____ / 26 Lower ____ / 26	
	Upper ____ / 26 Lower ____ / 26		Upper ____ / 26 Lower ____ / 26	
	Upper ____ / 26 Lower ____ / 26		Upper ____ / 26 Lower ____ / 26	
	Upper ____ / 26 Lower ____ / 26		Upper ____ / 26 Lower ____ / 26	
	Upper ____ / 26 Lower ____ / 26		Upper ____ / 26 Lower ____ / 26	

Sound Systems: Explicit, Systematic Phonics in Early Literacy Contexts by Anna Lyon and Paula Moore. Copyright © 2003. Stenhouse Publishers.

Class Phonics Profile

Grade _____   Teacher _____   Date _____

Name and Comments	READING		WRITING	
	Text Reading	Names Test	Writing Sample	Predicted Spelling Stage
Name: **Comments:**	Level: _____ Use of information:	Score: _____ / 70 Work needed on:	% Conventional Spelling _____ % Unconventional Spelling _____ Work needed on:	Stage: _____ Work needed on:
Name: **Comments:**	Level: _____ Use of information:	Score: _____ / 70 Work needed on:	% Conventional Spelling _____ % Unconventional Spelling _____ Work needed on:	Stage: _____ Work needed on:
Name: **Comments:**	Level: _____ Use of information:	Score: _____ / 70 Work needed on:	% Conventional Spelling _____ % Unconventional Spelling _____ Work needed on:	Stage: _____ Work needed on:

Phonics Development over Time
Individual Record Sheet for Grades Pre-K, K, and 1

Name: _____

Grade: _____

	Beginning of Year Date:	Mid Year Date:	End of Year Date:
Letter Names	# Uppercase Known ____ / 26 # Lowercase Known ____ / 26 Unknown/Confused:	# Uppercase Known ____ / 26 # Lowercase Known ____ / 26 Unknown/Confused:	# Uppercase Known ____ / 26 # Lowercase Known ____ / 26 Unknown/Confused:
Letter Sounds	# Uppercase Sounds Known ____ / 26 # Lowercase Sounds Known ____ / 26 Unknown/Confused:	# Uppercase Sounds Known ____ / 26 # Lowercase Sounds Known ____ / 26 Unknown/Confused:	# Uppercase Sounds Known ____ / 26 # Lowercase Sounds Known ____ / 26 Unknown/Confused:
Text Reading	Level: _____ Use of information:	Level: _____ Use of information:	Level: _____ Use of information:
Writing Sample	% Conventional Spelling ____ % Unconventional Spelling ____ Work needed on:	% Conventional Spelling ____ % Unconventional Spelling ____ Work needed on:	% Conventional Spelling ____ % Unconventional Spelling ____ Work needed on:
Predicted Spelling Stage	Stage: _____ Work needed on:	Stage: _____ Work needed on:	Stage: _____ Work needed on:

Phonics Development over Time
Individual Record Sheet for Grades 1, 2, and 3

Name: _____

Grade: _____

	Beginning of Year Date:	Mid Year Date:	End of Year Date:
Text Reading	Level: _____ Use of information:	Level: _____ Use of information:	Level: _____ Use of information:
Names Test	Score: _____ / 70 Work needed on:	Score: _____ / 70 Work needed on:	Score: _____ / 70 Work needed on:
Writing Sample	% Conventional Spelling _____ % Unconventional Spelling _____ Work needed on:	% Conventional Spelling _____ % Unconventional Spelling _____ Work needed on:	% Conventional Spelling _____ % Unconventional Spelling _____ Work needed on:
Predicted Spelling Stage	Stage: _____ Work needed on:	Stage: _____ Work needed on:	Stage: _____ Work needed on:

Record of Phonics Instruction in Reading
Emergent and Early/Letter-Name Development Stages (K–1)

Students _____

Categories	**Concepts Instructed and Date**

Initial Consonants
(e.g., <u>b</u>all, <u>l</u>ike, <u>m</u>e)

Final Consonants
(e.g., go<u>t</u>, bal<u>l</u>, slee<u>p</u>)

Initial Consonant Blends
(e.g., <u>st</u>op, <u>pl</u>ease, <u>bl</u>ack)

Initial Consonant Digraphs
(e.g., <u>sh</u>eep, <u>ch</u>ip, <u>th</u>is, <u>wh</u>en)

Short Vowels/Word Families
(e.g., b<u>ad</u>, l<u>et</u>, d<u>ig</u>)

Inflected Endings
(e.g., go<u>ing</u>, kick<u>ed</u>)

Final Consonant Blends
(e.g., hel<u>p</u>, du<u>mp</u>, po<u>nd</u>)

Final Consonant Digraphs
(e.g., mu<u>ch</u>, fi<u>sh</u>, ma<u>th</u>)

Record of Phonics Instruction in Reading
Early/Within-Word-Pattern and Transitional/Within-Word-Pattern Stages

Students_____

Categories	**Concepts Instructed and Date**
VCe Vowel Patterns (e.g., b<u>a</u>k<u>e</u>, k<u>i</u>t<u>e</u>, h<u>o</u>l<u>e</u>)	
CVVC Vowel Patterns (e.g., r<u>ai</u>n, sh<u>ee</u>p, c<u>oa</u>t)	
Other Long Vowel Patterns (e.g., n<u>igh</u>t, c<u>o</u>l<u>d</u>, bl<u>ue</u>, m<u>ay</u>)	
R-controlled Vowel Patterns (e.g., c<u>ar</u>, h<u>er</u>, f<u>ir</u>, f<u>or</u>, f<u>ur</u>)	
Abstract Vowel Patterns (e.g., b<u>oy</u>, b<u>oo</u>k, cl<u>own</u>)	
Complex Consonant Blends (e.g., <u>qu</u>iet, <u>scr</u>am, <u>thr</u>ew)	
Hard and Soft c & g (e.g., cell/call, rag/rage)	
Silent Consonants (e.g., com<u>b</u>, <u>w</u>rite, <u>k</u>now)	
Sounds for *ed* (e.g., lifted, rained, asked)	
Homophones (e.g., their/there, hear/here)	
Homographs (e.g., read/read)	
Contractions (e.g., you're, she'd, let's)	

Record of Phonics Instruction in Reading
Transitional/Syllable-Juncture Stage

Students _____

Categories	**Concepts Instructed and Date**
Compound Words (e.g., bookcase, twenty-five)	
Doubling Consonant (e.g., bat/batted)	
Dropping *e* (e.g., hope/hoping)	
Open Syllable Patterns (e.g., pi•rate, o•pen, rea•son)	
Closed Syllable Patterns (e.g., en•ter, bas•ket, but•ter)	
Syllable Stress (e.g., un•HAPPY, MAIN•ly)	
Plurals (e.g., dogs, beaches, ponies)	
Possessives (e.g., boy's/boys')	
Prefixes (e.g., dislike, misfit, refill)	
Suffixes (e.g., cheerful, likely, sickness)	

Record of Whole-Group Phonics Instruction in Writing Emergent and Early/Letter-Name Development Stages (K–1)

Categories	Concepts Instructed and Date
Initial Consonants (e.g., <u>b</u>all, <u>l</u>ike, <u>m</u>e)	
Final Consonants (e.g., go<u>t</u>, bal<u>l</u>, slee<u>p</u>)	
Initial Consonant Blends (e.g., <u>st</u>op, <u>pl</u>ease, <u>bl</u>ack)	
Initial Consonant Digraphs (e.g., <u>sh</u>eep, <u>ch</u>ip, <u>th</u>is, <u>wh</u>en)	
Short Vowels/Word Families (e.g., b<u>ad</u>, l<u>et</u>, d<u>ig</u>)	
Inflected Endings (e.g., go<u>ing</u>, kick<u>ed</u>)	
Final Consonant Blends (e.g., he<u>lp</u>, du<u>mp</u>, po<u>nd</u>)	
Final Consonant Digraphs (e.g., mu<u>ch</u>, fi<u>sh</u>, ma<u>th</u>)	

Sound Systems: Explicit, Systematic Phonics in Early Literacy Contexts by Anna Lyon and Paula Moore. Copyright © 2003. Stenhouse Publishers.

Record of Whole-Group Phonics Instruction in Writing
Early/Within-Word-Pattern and Transitional/Within-Word-Pattern Stages

Categories	Concepts Instructed and Date
VCe Vowel Patterns (e.g., b<u>ake</u>, k<u>ite</u>, h<u>ole</u>)	
CVVC Vowel Patterns (e.g., r<u>ain</u>, sh<u>eep</u>, c<u>oat</u>)	
Other Long Vowel Patterns (e.g., n<u>ight</u>, c<u>old</u>, bl<u>ue</u>, m<u>ay</u>)	
R-controlled Vowel Patterns (e.g., c<u>ar</u>, h<u>er</u>, f<u>ir</u>, f<u>or</u>, f<u>ur</u>)	
Abstract Vowel Patterns (e.g., b<u>oy</u>, b<u>ook</u>, cl<u>own</u>)	
Complex Consonant Blends (e.g., <u>qu</u>iet, <u>scr</u>am, <u>thr</u>ew)	
Hard and Soft c & g (e.g., cell/call, rag/rage)	
Silent Consonants (e.g., com<u>b</u>, <u>w</u>rite, <u>k</u>now)	
Sounds for *ed* (e.g., lifted, rained, asked)	
Homophones (e.g., their/there, hear/here)	
Homographs (e.g., read/read)	
Contractions (e.g., you're, she'd, let's)	

Record of Whole-Group Phonics Instruction in Writing
Transitional/Syllable-Juncture Stage

Categories	Concepts Instructed and Date

Compound Words
(e.g., bookcase, twenty-five)

Doubling Consonant
(e.g., bat/batted)

Dropping e
(e.g., hope/hoping)

Open Syllable Patterns
(e.g., pi•rate, o•pen, rea•son)

Closed Syllable Patterns
(e.g., en•ter, bas•ket, but•ter)

Syllable Stress
(e.g., un•HAPPY, MAIN•ly)

Plurals
(e.g., dogs, beaches, ponies)

Possessives
(e.g., boy's/boys')

Prefixes
(e.g., dislike, misfit, refill)

Suffixes
(e.g., cheerful, likely, sickness)

Sound Systems: Explicit, Systematic Phonics in Early Literacy Contexts by Anna Lyon and Paula Moore. Copyright © 2003. Stenhouse Publishers.

Appendix H

Resources for Teachers

To keep abreast of high-quality children's books visit the following web sites. Lists can be downloaded or purchased for a small fee.

www.ncte.org/elem/pictus
This site lists winners of the prestigious Orbis Pictus award for quality nonfiction children's literature.

www.ala.org/alsc/newberry.html
Newberry Medal winners from 1922 through 2002 are listed.

www.ala.org/alsc/caldecott.html
Caldecott Medal winners from 1938 through 2002 are listed. The site also links to the Coretta Scott King Award site.

www.ala.org/booklist/v94/002.org
This site offers lists of quality children's fiction and nonfiction books.

www.naeyc.org
Brochures can be purchased for a small fee. Titles include: "Books to Grow On: African American Literature for Young Children" (No. 568) and "Books to Grow On: Latino Literature for Young Children" (No. 581).

www.reading.org
The International Reading Association lists Children's Choices books. Be sure to visit the list for beginning and young readers. Songs and nursery rhymes can be previewed, downloaded, and/or purchased through the following web sites:

www.acs.vcalgary.html
This site includes book lists, songs, and poems.

www.geocities.com/EnchantedForest/Glade/7438/index.html
Mother Goose nursery rhymes and songs that teach are included at this site. Words to the songs can be downloaded.

www.bobbysussersongs.com
Bobby Susser's songs teach children about letter sounds, colors, seasons, and friendship.

www.theteachersguide.com/childrensSongs.html
This site includes a wide variety of songs for teachers to use in classrooms.

www.kiddles.com/index.html
Songs that teach such as AlphaSongs by Greg Whitfield are featured at this site.

These books suggest classroom activities to use as children learn phonemic awareness and phonics. Some are accompanied by sing-along audiocassettes.

Ayres, M. J., and L. Brain. 1997. *Natural Learning from A–Z: Phonemic Awareness Emphasis for Letters and Letter Sounds.* Leland, MS: Natural Learning Publications.

Blevens, W. 1991. *Phonemic Awareness Songs and Rhymes.* New York: Scholastic. (book and tape)

Fitzpatrick, J., R. Drew, and T. Peterson. 1997. *Phonemic Awareness: Playing with Sounds to Strengthen Beginning Reading Skills.* Cypress, CA: Creative Teaching Press.

Love, E. 1996. *Sound Way: Phonics Activities for Early Literacy.* Markham, ON, Canada: Pembroke Publishers.

Traugh, S. 1991. Fun Phonics Series. Cypress, CA: Creative Teaching Press. (books and tapes)

Sample Schedule for All-Day Kindergarten

8:00–8:30	Opening activities and read aloud
8:30–9:00	Circle time (shared reading, shared writing, songs, or learning games and activities)
9:00–10:00	Centers (math, science, social studies, art, blocks, language arts, etc.). The teacher will use this time to interact with the children at centers or to call small groups together for instruction.
10:00–10:30	Snack and recess
10:30–11:15	Math activities
11:15–12:00	Special classes (art, music, PE, media)
12:00–12:30	Lunch
12:30–1:00	Science/social studies
1:00–1:45	Free-choice play at housekeeping, block, and other centers
1:45–2:00	Circle time to recap the day/preview tomorrow

Templates for Masks

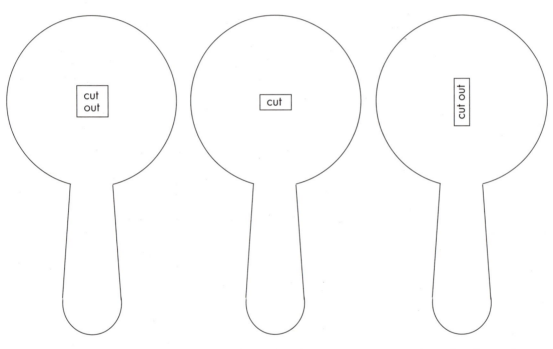

Use to frame letters
in big books

Use to frame high-frequency
words in text

Use to frame cap letters, letters
with descenders (g, j, p, q, y),
or letters with ascenders
(b, d, f, h, k, l, t)

Sound Systems: Explicit, Systematic Phonics in Early Literacy Contexts by Anna Lyon and Paula Moore. Copyright © 2003. Stenhouse Publishers.

Making and Using a Sliding Mask

For use primarily to help the student locate familiar items of print, such as initial letters and known words, or to analyze new words or word parts for study.

While this momentary and occasional isolation of letter or word can be done at any time during the lesson, it is probably most useful after reading a book.

Directions:

1. Glue two six-by-four-inch cards along the top and bottom.

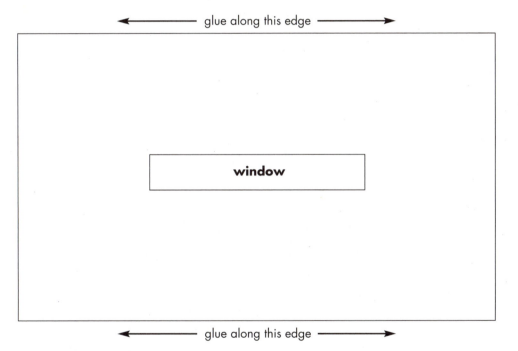

glue along this edge

window

glue along this edge

2. Cut a half-inch high by two-and-a-half-inch wide window in the center.

3. Glue two eight-by-two-inch strips of card stock (for strength) together. Check to make sure the strip slides freely over the window.

References

Professional Books

Adams, M. 1990. *Beginning to Read: Thinking and Learning About Print.* Cambridge, MA: MIT Press.

Adams, M., B. Foorman, I. Lundberg, and T. Beeler. 1998. *Phonemic Awareness in Young Children.* Baltimore: Paul H. Brookes.

Bailey, M. H. 1967. "The Utility of Phonic Generalizations in Grades One Through Six." *Reading Teacher* 20: 413–418.

Bear, D., M. Invernizzi, S. Templeton, and F. Johnston. 2000. *Words Their Way: Word Study for Phonics, Vocabulary, and Spelling Instruction.* Upper Saddle River, NJ: Merrill, an imprint of Prentice-Hall.

Bear, D., P. Truex, and D. Barone. 1989. "In Search of Meaningful Diagnosis: Spelling-by-Stage Assessment of Literacy Proficiency." *Adult Literacy and Basic Education* 13 (3): 165–185.

Beers, J. 1980. "Developmental Strategies of Spelling Competence in Primary School Children." In E. H. Henderson and J. W. Beers, eds., *Cognitive and Developmental Aspects of Learning to Spell: A Reflection of Word Knowledge.* Newark, DE: International Reading Association.

Beers, J., and E. Henderson. 1977. "A Study of Developing Orthographic Concepts Among First Graders." *Research in the Teaching of English* 2: 133–148.

Berdiansky, B., B. Cronnell, and J. Koehler. 1969. *Spelling-Sound Relations and Primary Form-Class Descriptions for Speech Comprehension Vocabularies of 6–9 Year Olds.* Technical report no. 15. Los Alamitos, CA: Southwest Regional Laboratory for Educational Research and Development.

Bowman, B. T., M. S. Donovan, and M. S. Burns, eds. 2001. *Eager to Learn: Educating Our Preschoolers.* Washington, DC: National Academy Press.

Bransford, J., A. Brown, and R. Cocking, eds. 1999. *How People Learn: Brain, Mind, Experience, and School.* National Research Council. Washington, DC: National Academy Press.

Burmeister, L. E. 1968. "Usefulness of Phonic Generalizations." *Reading Teacher* 21: 349–356.

Burns, M. S., P. Griffin, and C. E. Snow, eds. 1999. *Starting Out Right: A Guide to Promoting Children's Reading Success.* Washington, DC: National Academy Press.

Clay, M. 1991. *Becoming Literate: The Construction of Inner Control.* Portsmouth, NH: Heinemann.

———. 1993. *An Observation Survey of Early Literacy Achievement.* Portsmouth, NH: Heinemann.

———. 1998. *By Different Paths to Common Outcomes.* Portland, ME: Stenhouse.

———. 2000. *Running Records for Classroom Teachers.* Portsmouth, NH: Heinemann.

———. 2001. *Change Over Time in Children's Literacy Development.* Portsmouth, NH: Heinemann.

Clymer, T. 1963. "The Utility of Phonic Generalizations in the Primary Grades." *Reading Teacher* 16: 252–258.

Cunningham, P. M. 1990. "The Names Test: A Quick Assessment of Decoding Ability." *Reading Teacher* 44: 124–129.

———. 1995. *Phonics They Use: Words for Reading and Writing,* 2d ed. New York: HarperCollins College Publisher.

Dahl, K. L., O. L. Scharer, L. L. Lawson, and P. R. Grogan. 2001. *Rethinking Phonics: Making the Best Teaching Decisions.* Portsmouth, NH: Heinemann.

Dorn, L., C. French, and T. Jones. 1998. *Apprenticeship in Literacy: Transitions Across Reading and Writing.* Portland, ME: Stenhouse.

Dorn, L., and C. Soffos. 2001. *Shaping Literate Minds: Developing Self-Regulated Learners.* Portland, ME: Stenhouse.

Duffelmeyer, F. A., A. E. Kruse, D. J. Merkley, and S. A. Fyfe. 1994. "Further Validation and Enhancement of the Names Test." *Reading Teacher* 48 (2): 118–128.

Ehri, L., and L. Wilce. 1985. "Do Beginners Learn to Read Function Words Better in Sentences or in Lists?" *Reading Research Quarterly* 20: 163–179.

Emans, R. 1967. "The Usefulness of Phonic Generalizations Above the Primary Grades." *Reading Teacher* 20: 419–425.

Ferreiro, E., and A. Teberosky. 1982. *Literacy Before Schooling.* Portsmouth, NH: Heinemann.

Fountas, I. C., and G. S. Pinnell. 1996. *Guided Reading: Good First Teaching for All Children.* Portsmouth, NH: Heinemann.

———. 1999. *Matching Books to Readers: Using Leveled Books in Guided Reading K–3.* Portsmouth, NH: Heinemann.

———. 2001. *Guiding Readers and Writers Grades 3–6: Teaching Comprehension, Genre, and Content Literacy.* Portsmouth, NH: Heinemann.

Fox, B. J. 2000. *Word Identification Strategies: Phonics from a New Perspective,* 2d ed. Upper Saddle River, NJ: Merrill, an imprint of Prentice-Hall.

Ganske, K. 2000. *Word Journeys: Assessment-Guided Phonics, Spelling, and Vocabulary Instruction.* New York: The Guilford Press.

Gentry, J. R. 1980. "Three Steps to Teaching Beginning Readers to Spell." In E. H. Henderson and J. W. Beers, eds., *Cognitive and Developmental Aspects of Learning to Spell: A Reflection of Word Knowledge.* Newark, DE: International Reading Association.

Goswami, U. 1986. *Phonological Skills and Learning to Read.* Hillsdale, NJ: Lawrence Erlbaum.

Henderson, E. 1990. *Teaching Spelling* (rev. ed.). Boston: Houghton Mifflin.

Henderson, E., T. Estes, and S. Stonecase. 1972. "An Exploratory Study of Word Acquisition Among First Graders at Midyear in a Language-Experience Approach." *Journal of Reading Behavior* 4 (3): 21–31.

Henderson, L. 1984. *Orthographies and Reading.* Hillsdale, NJ: Lawrence Erlbaum.

Holdaway, D. 1979. *The Foundations of Literacy.* Portsmouth, NH: Heinemann.

Horn, E. 1929. "The Child's Early Experience with the Letter *a.*" *Journal of Educational Psychology* 20: 161–168.

Hull, M. A., and M. J. Fox. 1998. *Phonics for the Teacher of Reading.* Upper Saddle River, NJ: Merrill, an imprint of Prentice-Hall.

Invernizzi, M., M. Abouzeid, and J. T. Gill. 1994. "Using Students' Invented Spellings as a Guide for Spelling Instruction That Emphasizes Word Study." *The Elementary School Journal* 95 (2): 155–167.

McCarrier, A., I. Fountas, and G. S. Pinnell. 2000. *Interactive Writing: How Language and Literacy Come Together, K–2.* Portsmouth, NH: Heinemann.

Miller, G. A. 1956. "The Magical Number Seven, Plus or Minus Two: Some Limits on Our Capacity for Processing Information." *Psychological Review* 63: 81–97.

Moats, L. 1995. *Spelling Development, Disability, and Instruction.* Baltimore: York Press.

Mooney, M. 1990. *Reading To, With, and by Children.* Katonah, NY: Richard C. Owen.

Moustafa, M. 1997. *Beyond Traditional Phonics: Research Discoveries and Reading Instruction.* Portsmouth, NH: Heinemann.

National Institute of Child Health and Human Development (NICHHD). (December 2000a). Report of the National Reading Panel. Teaching children to read: An evidence-based assessment of the scientific research literature on reading and its implications for reading instruction. (NIH Pub No. 00-4769). Washington, DC: Author.

———. (December 2000b). Report of the National Reading Panel, Reports of the Subgroups. Teaching children to read: An evidence-based assessment of the scientific research literature on reading and its implications for reading instruction. (NIH Pub No. 00-4754). Washington, DC: Author.

New Standards Primary Committee. 1999. *Reading and Writing Grade by Grade: Primary Literacy Standards for Kindergarten Through Third Grade.* Pittsburgh, PA: National Center on Education and the Economy and the University of Pittsburgh.

New Zealand Ministry of Education. 1994. *Reading in Junior Classes.* Katonah, NY: Richard C. Owen.

Parkes, B. 2000. *Read It Again! Revisiting Shared Reading.* Portland, ME: Stenhouse.

Pinnell, G. S., and I. C. Fountas. 1998. *Word Matters: Teaching Phonics and Spelling in the Reading/Writing Classroom.* Portsmouth, NH: Heinemann.

Read, C. 1971. "Pre-School Children's Knowledge of English Phonology." *Harvard Educational Review* 41 (1): 150–179.

———. 1975. *Children's Categorization of Speech Sounds in English.* Urbana, IL: National Council of Teachers of English.

Schlagal, R. 1989. "Constancy and Change in Spelling Development." *Reading Psychology* 10 (3): 207–229.

Snow, C. E., M. S. Burns, and P. Griffin, eds. 1998. *Preventing Reading Difficulties in Young Children.* Washington, DC: National Academy Press.

Spector, J. 1992. "Predicting Progress in Beginning Reading: Dynamic Assessment of Phonemic Awareness." *Journal of Educational Psychology* 84: 353–363.

Strickland, D. 1998. *Teaching Phonics Today: A Primer for Educators*. Newark, DE: International Reading Association.

Strickland, D., and L. Morrow, eds. 1989. *Emerging Literacy: Young Children Learn to Read and Write*. Newark, DE: International Reading Association.

Teale, W. H., and E. Sulzby, eds. 1986. *Emergent Literacy: Writing and Reading*. Norwood, NJ: Ablex.

Templeton, S. 1983. "Using the Spelling/Meaning Connection to Develop Word Knowledge in Older Students." *Journal of Reading* 27: 8–14.

Tunmer, W. E., and A. R. Nesdale. 1985. "Phonemic Segmentation Skill and Beginning Reading." *Journal of Educational Psychology* 77: 417–427.

Wilde, S. 1997. *What's a Schwa Sound Anyway? A Holistic Guide to Phonetics, Phonics, and Spelling*. Portsmouth, NH: Heinemann.

Wood, D. 1996. *How Children Think and Learn*. Cambridge, MA: Blackwell.

Zutell, J. 1996. "The Directed Spelling Thinking Activity (DSTA): Providing an Effective Balance in Word Study Instruction." *Reading Teacher* 50 (2): 98–108.

Children's Books

Brown, M. W. 1975. *Goodnight Moon*. Pictures by Clement Hurd. New York: Harper & Row.

Cowley, J. 1988. *The Jigaree*. Illustrations by Deirdre Gardiner. Bothell, WA: Wright Group.

———. 1990. *Mrs. Wishy Washy*. Bothell, WA: Wright Group.

———. 1998. *Dishy-Washy*. Bothell, WA: Wright Group.

Kennedy, X. J., and D. M. Kennedy. 1992. *Talking Like the Rain: A Read-to-Me Book of Poems*. Illustrations by Jane Dyer. New York: Little, Brown.

Martin, B., Jr. 1996. *Brown Bear, Brown Bear*. New York: Henry Holt.

Mead, K. 1998. *The Missing Pet*. Illustrations by Judith DuFour Love. Austin, TX: Steck-Vaughn.

Melser, J. 1981. *My Home*. Illustrations by Isabel Lowe. Bothwell, WA: Wright Group.

Owens, J. 1992. *One Sock, Two Socks*. Illustrations by Michael Martchenko. Carlsbad, CA: Dominie Press.

Parkes, B. 1996. *Who's in the Shed?* Crystal Lake, IL: Rigby.

———. 1998. *The Royal Dinner*. Crystal Lake, IL: Rigby.

Parkes, B., and J. Smith. 1986. *The Gingerbread Man*. Crystal Lake, IL: Rigby.

Polacco, P. 1993. *Babushka Baba Yaga*. New York: Penguin Putnam Books for Young Readers.

———. 1994. *My Rotten Redheaded Older Brother*. New York: Simon & Schuster Books for Young Readers.

Randell, B. 1996a. *Baby Lamb's First Drink*. Illustrations by Ernest Papps. Petone, NZ: Nelson Price Milburn Ltd. Distributed in the United States by Rigby under the PM Story Books collection.

———. 1996b. *Mushrooms for Dinner*. Illustrations by Isabel Lowe. Petone, NZ: Nelson Price Milburn Ltd. Distributed in the United States by Rigby under the PM Story Books collection.

Scieszka, J. 1989. *The True Story of the Three Little Pigs.* Illustrations by Lane Smith. New York: Viking.

Swartz, S. L. 1997. *Crabs, Shrimp, and Lobsters.* Photography by Robert Yin. Carlsbad, CA: Dominie Press.

Westcott, N. B. 1987. *Peanut Butter and Jelly: A Play Rhyme.* New York: Viking Penguin.

Wilhelm, J. 1998. *Our Dad.* Cambridge, MA: Educators Publishing Service.

Index

abstract vowels, 15, 123
affixes, 16, 125
affricate, 14, 113
alphabet books, 98
analogy, use of, 12
assessment, 8. *See also* phonics assessment; writing sample analysis

c, hard and soft, 15
class phonics profile
    explanation of, 57–58
    forms for, 142, 143
    in-depth, 58–60
classrooms
    fostering instructional methods, 72
    print-rich, 70
closed syllables, 16, 124
compound words, 16, 124
consonant blends, 15
consonant digraphs, 15
consonants
    doubling, 16, 125
    explanation of, 15, 121, 122
    initial, 120
    silent, 15
content area study, 71–72, 114
contractions, 16, 123
curriculum
    in design of phonics programs, 8
    developmental phonics, 17–21
    instruction and, 116–118
    using student performance to assess, 64–65

derivational-constancy errors, 45
Developmental Spelling Inventory (DSI), 53
developmental stages, errors beyond estimated, 45, 47–51, 55

doubling consonants, 16, 125
Dynamic Assessment of Phonemic Awareness
    explanation of, 33–34, 129–130
    introductory instructions to students and, 130–131
    response sheet for, 132

e, dropping, 16, 125
early/letter-name stage
    analysis of errors on running records for, 126
    analysis of errors on writing samples for, 139
    explanation of, 120
    record of phonics instruction in reading for, 146
    record of whole-group phonics instruction in writing for, 149
early readers
    experiences of, 13
    explanation of, 11–12, 18
early stage
    accommodating individual differences in, 97–102
    classroom schedule for, 91–93
    instructional context for how words work, 96–97
    instructional context for teaching phonics in reading in, 93–94
    phonics use in spelling and writing in, 94–95
early/within-word-pattern stage
    analysis of errors on running records for, 127
    analysis of errors on writing samples for, 140
    explanation of, 121
    record of phonics instruction in reading for, 147
    record of whole-group phonics instruction in writing for, 150